The Flipside of Fear

Finding Freedom Where You Least Expect It

David Ronka

CLIFFHOUSE PRESS

Cover design by Katie Atkinson
Author photograph by Jay Schadler

ISBN-13: 978-1-7320033-4-7

DOWNLOAD THE FLIPSIDE WORKSHEET, A FREE TOOL TO HELP YOU WORK THROUGH THE PROCESS DESCRIBED IN THIS BOOK.

To download, go to:
www.davidronka.com/the-flipside-of-fear

Everything you've ever wanted
is on the other side of fear.

–George Addair

Contents

Introduction

So there are two ways you can live:
you can devote your life to
staying in your comfort zone,
or you can work on your freedom.
–Michael Singer

Fear is Everywhere

Fear is all around us. It's the water in which we swim. Newscasters thrive on reporting all the ways the world is falling apart. It sometimes seems like fear is at the heart of every conversation around us. For many of us, fear is in our blood. It lurks in the shadows when we face a big decision, an important conversation, or when we try to step beyond our comfort zone.

Perhaps if you're like me, life didn't start that way. There were big dreams, inspired decisions, and courageous steps, but somewhere along the way something happened. The first half of life was spent building and pursuing—a career, a family, and all the stuff I wanted to have—and I was pretty good at it.

But then I woke up one day in mid-life with the sinking feeling that something wasn't right. I was going through the motions in my personal and professional life, and I'd lost my sense of passion and purpose. I couldn't imagine another 30, 40, or 50 years of living like that.

What happens when we reach this point in life? It's terrifying to realize we're not who, what, or where we thought we'd be, and that the rules we were taught to live by—that governed the first half of life—no longer work for us. But when we want to break out of the mold, we find limits—limits governed by fear. Maybe you can relate to one or more of these limits:

- You want to step away from an uninspiring job and pursue your passion full-time . . . but you fear you won't make it on your own, and/or you don't know HOW.

- You've been alone for too long, and you want to find a partner with whom you can share your life . . . but you fear rejection.

- You want to try something new . . . but you fear looking and/or feeling like a failure.

- You want to do something for *you* . . . but you fear disappointing others and/or yourself.

- You want to follow that feeling in your heart that says you're made for something more, something bigger . . . but you fear stepping into the unknown.

If you struggle with fear, you might relate. Fear is everywhere, and fear can be debilitating. It can show up anytime—even when the grass is green, the sky is blue, and everyone around you is smiling and laughing.

This book is for those of us who can't get rid of self-limiting voices in the head—*you can't do that, say that, have that, be that.* This book is for those of us who are tired of being held back and limited by their fears. This book is for those of us who are ready to step into a re-energized abundant life, free and clear.

Stop Fighting Your Fear

I'm not going to tell you how to get rid of your fears. In fact, I'm going to show you how **your fear is actually your ally.** You see, all along your fear has been trying to protect you. What we might call the "front side" of fear—pit in the stomach, voices in the head, panic attacks, frantic activity, paralysis—is our fear's way of alerting us to and trying to keep us out of danger. However, most of those dangers are *perceived* dangers, not real dangers, the seeds of which were sewn in childhood or through painful life lessons or from the warnings of others.

If you recognize and approach your fear and learn to harness its energy, you can emerge into the "flipside" of fear. Each of your fears, once explored and understood, carries with it the compass and the power to direct and propel you into the life you've dreamed of living.

In *The Flipside of Fear*, I'll show you a straightforward three-step process for transforming your fears into freedom. It all boils down to this:

1. **Interrupt your fear** by stopping your natural, knee-jerk reactions which keep you living in the same rut, day in and day out.

2. **Approach your fear** by getting curious about the "belief ecosystem" that drives your fear and what your fear has been trying to protect you from.

3. **Flip your fear** by identifying a new way of living that's aligned with who you want to be.

While this process is straightforward, it's not so easy. If it were, we'd all be living fulfilling, satisfying lives.

My Flipside

I'm writing this book because I've been through a life-changing process with my own fear. And I've seen many of my friends and colleagues bravely approach their fear and emerge on the flipside, inspired and equipped to live more fully. I'm writing this book because I want to accompany you as you experience this same transformation—from fear to freedom.

I spent my 20s, 30s, and early 40s trapped by fear. I was in a career that had at one point inspired me but had become frustrating and numbing with excessive travel, long hours, and very little use of my creativity. I was afraid to step away from the security of a corporate job, the promise of a big payout at retirement, and the expectations of those around me.

I grew up in a religious tradition that had at one point energized me but had lost its power to transform my life and make a real difference. I was afraid to turn away from the traditions and dogma of my youth and venture into new spiritual territories.

I was in a 15-year marriage that was "good enough" but lacked passion and forward movement despite years of therapy, self-reflection, and effort on both sides. I was afraid to even consider the big D-word, thinking that love meant sticking it out regardless.

I used to enjoy traveling and seeking adventure, but a traumatic flight left me with anxiety every time I needed to step foot on an airplane, robbing me of my passion for new experiences.

And I could give so many other examples of how my fear created a straightjacket of limitations, within which I felt trapped and helpless.

However, I have learned how to recognize fear when it shows up, approach it and explore it, and find the flipside—that new way of being that fulfills my life purpose and fills me with passion. That's not to say that I no longer experience fear. Rather, dealing productively with my fear has become a regular practice in my life.

I've moved through my fears in each of those areas where fear plagued me. And I've found the flipside:

- non-traditional work that gives me diversity, choice, flexibility, an outlet for my creativity, and space in my schedule;

- a spiritual practice that keeps me connected to God and to myself in ways I'd never before experienced;

- a relationship with a woman I love, who loves me, and with whom I easily create and manifest life dreams; and

- a sense of peace and calm when I'm in flight, re-igniting my travel bug and freeing me to explore our world.

And each new fear that comes up (there seem to be less of them now) has the potential to add to and deepen my flipside.

Action Over Analysis

This isn't a book full of research and analysis. There are already lots of those out there, and many of them are quite helpful. Rather, I've tried to write a down-to-earth resource for those who want to find relief from their fears **right now**.

I know this can happen because I'm a living, breathing, walking example. But this isn't just my personal claim. The growing field of neuroscience has introduced the concept of "neuroplasticity," which reverses the previously-held belief that our brains are basically fixed after adolescence. What does this mean for you and me? It means that we can grow and change. We can get un-stuck.

If this is what you want, then this book is for you. I'll share with you how I first discovered my fears as they ran wild with my thoughts and beliefs. And I'll share with you the process I've used for achieving freedom from debilitating, knee-jerk reactions and for inviting fear to a different agenda, an inspired way of being—to the flipside.

You'll find practical exercises you can do on a daily basis to help build your ability to live on the flipside, as well as examples of what this looks like. I'll show you a path for how to go from limited, fear-based living to in-spired, open-hearted living where you are the master of your own destiny and can create any reality you can dream of.

In Chapter 1 we'll explore the nature of fear, how to recognize it when it shows up, and the ways in which it limits us. In Chapter 2 we'll look at the flipside of fear—how to uncover it and live into it. In Chapters 3, 4, and 5 we'll dig into each step of the process with examples and exercises you can do to practice the steps. And in Chap-ter 6 we'll discover how to live on the flipside of fear—day in, day out. Rather than interrupt the flow of the book with footnotes, I've included extra information that I think might be helpful in endnotes. None of the end-notes are critical for understanding the book.

It's Your Time to Live!

If you practice the steps outlined in this book, you will experience immediate relief from your fear and you will begin to see new opportunities opening up around you. It's my hope that you'll learn to harness the wisdom and power that comes from moving through your fear and that you'll confidently emerge into the light of freedom.

Please don't wait! You have so many gifts to give to the world. Don't let fear hold you back. You have too many dreams for the future. Don't let fear limit your potential. You have a great, great capacity to give and receive love. Don't let fear close you down.

The process you're about to learn can open a whole new world for you. Read on to reignite that sense of eager anticipation that you had before your fears took over. Rediscover what it's like to be confident and clear. Rewrite the script of your life. Join me and learn how to get unstuck, expand your comfort zone, and find the life-giving force hidden in every fear.

CHAPTER 1

Exploring Fear

The fears we don't face become our limits.
−Robin Sharma

What is Fear?

I f you look up the definition of fear, you'll see some basic themes: fear is an emotion or feeling; fear is unpleasant and uncomfortable; fear is caused by real or perceived danger. In my experience, fear is also sneaky. We can catch glimpses of it, and we can certainly feel the debilitating effects of it. However, I've found it difficult to see its true nature because when fear arises, the last thing I want do is cozy up to it.

In this first chapter, I'd like to shine a spotlight on the nature of fear. Of course, every specific fear has its own personality—its own special ways of scaring us into submission. However, I think we can learn something useful by taking a step back and trying to discover the look and feel of fear in general.

Let's start with this: fear is an emotion. You may have heard that there are four basic emotions: anger, sadness, fear, and gladness. That's one way to look at it. In my experience, however, there are really only two basic emotions. There's fear and there's love. Everything in between is some combination of the two.[1]

Put simply, fear is that which closes us down, and love is that which opens us up. When we're closed down—in fear—we're susceptible to negative emotions such as anger, blame, jealousy, worry, doubt, insecurity, guilt, despair, depression, and hopelessness. And when we're opened up—in love—we experience positive emotions such as joy, peace, passion, enthusiasm, empowerment, happiness, and contentment. **Finding the flipside of fear is all about moving from being closed down to being opened up.**

Appropriate Fear Keeps Us Alive

But that's not easy, especially since we're wired for fear. In our evolutionary past, fear kept us alive. Rick Hansen, in his book *Hardwiring Happiness*, writes that our brains have been wired to be on a constant lookout for fear. He posits that we are ten times more likely to notice danger than we are likely to notice non-danger. The reason for this is clear: noticing danger kept the human species alive and evolving—miss the lion in the bush and it's all over; miss the tasty blueberry patch and you'll likely live another day to find another tasty blueberry patch.

Fear is what alerts us to dangers that threaten us and then prepares us to deal with those dangers by equipping our bodies to react to the threat. Social scientists and biologists tell us there are three primary ways our bodies react to an immediate threat: fight, flight, or freeze (I recently heard someone add a fourth option: faint). In the moment of threat, our bodies shut down or diminish all unnecessary functions and processes to get maximum output for fighting, fleeing, or freezing.

In very basic terms (keeping in mind I'm not a biologist or social scientist), we have two types of nervous systems: the sympathetic nervous system (SNS) and the parasympathetic nervous system (PNS). The PNS is responsible for regulating long-term recovery states of being, such as rest and digestion. The SNS, on the other hand, is responsible for regulating the body's short-term response to perceived threats. Fear activates the SNS to get us into our survival state. Please take note of this distinction—I'll be getting back to it later.

You might even say that fear is our friend. This might sound ridiculous at first—it certainly doesn't feel that way most of the time. Without caution, which could be called *appropriate* fear, we might blissfully and cluelessly wander into situations that are best left alone: crossing the highway on foot to get to the Dunkin' Donuts; climbing over the fence at the zoo to pet the cute baby mountain lions; taking the casserole dish out of the

450° oven bare-handed because we can't be bothered with the oven mitt. You get the idea.

Inappropriate Fear Paralyzes and Limits Us

But what about when *inappropriate* fears show up in our lives? Regularly. Every day. That's another story. I recently realized that I spend a whole lot of time and energy trying to maintain a sense of comfort, stability, and security. In fact, if I'm not conscious and aware, the choices I make are largely guided by these basic, primal desires. Anything that threatens my comfort, stability, or security is identified by my psyche as enemy of the state. And what follows is a series of actions and moves that I've developed over time to defeat the enemy so that I can continue on in bliss.

These are *inappropriate* fears, and they can be debilitating. What I'm afraid of—the loss of comfort, stability, and security—are not actually life-threatening situations. In fact, sometimes it's *good* to feel uncomfortable, unstable, and insecure. In my experience, those feelings are often signals that I'm approaching my growth edge— that place right beyond my comfort zone—and they remind me that I need to lean into my edge, rather than shrink back. **My fear keeps me in a constant state of trying to avoid the very situations that can lead to my growth and expansion, leaving me in a straight-jacket of limited potential.**

When Thoughts Trigger Fear

This kind of fear—the fear that trips us up at just the moment we're trying to live boldly—is often triggered by our thoughts. Something we're doing (or considering doing) is in conflict with our self-limiting belief ecosystem. This ecosystem was developed over years and years of nurture—we internalized our parents' criticism; we loved someone and then were rejected; we took a risk and failed. Whatever the circumstances that have led to your unique belief ecosystem, we all have one, and it gets activated when we start approaching the growth edge.

Let me give an example of how I ran headlong into my belief ecosystem. I was stumbling my way through mid-life, post-divorce dating. I made mistakes, saw my old patterns show up, and wasn't always judicious in choosing my partners. But I was learning and growing.

Emotionally exhausted, I took a half year hiatus from dating. I used that time to reflect on what I really wanted in a relationship, and at the end of the six months, I wrote a very specific list of what I believed a "conscious relationship" would look like. Within weeks, and to my delight, I met a woman who had the same vision for a relationship.

She lived in the same town as I did, and I was thoroughly enjoying the free and easy nature of dating locally (all my recent relationships had been some form of long distance). We were getting to know each other, and I loved what I was experiencing. Our relationship was deepening, and for the first time post-divorce, I wasn't cringing when talking about anything beyond the next month. I even began calling her "my girlfriend," a term I had avoided in past relationships because it felt juvenile to me. In short, I was falling in love, and it felt great.

One warm summer evening we were relaxing at a beach near our town in New Hampshire, and she mentioned how much she'd like to live on the ocean. We both had been practicing manifestation (the art of creating in your life what you desire in your heart), so we decided to get serious (and playful) about it by dreaming about what that might look and feel like.[2]

A few months after our dreaming session on the beach, we were driving along the Maine coast and she casually pointed out a for rent sign on a house overlooking the ocean. It took our breath away: it was a three-story colonial perched on a small cliff overlooking the same waterway as the beach from a few months earlier, but from Maine rather than New Hampshire (a river separates the two states at that location). The more we thought about it—and we toured it several times—the more we loved it. We saw it as a direct manifestation of that dreaming session on the beach.

Moving in together was suddenly on the table. It wasn't something we'd yet considered, and now we found ourselves talking seriously about cohabitating. This represented a huge step forward for both of us, and I knew it was a moment of significant potential for growth—individually and for us as a couple. I was ready to commit to deepening the relationship, and this was an opportunity to move in that direction.

We were both feeling very positive about our relationship, and we felt buoyed by the vision of living together in this new, incredible space. So we called the landlord, said yes, and the next day I kissed her goodbye and got into my car to drive to Pennsylvania to spend Thanksgiving with family.

Then the fear hit. In about twelve hours I went from flying high with elation to curling into the fetal fear position. I was driving through Connecticut when I started to shut down. It was as if a vicious storm had whipped up out of nowhere, and my sunny, clear mindscape was replaced with roiling thunderheads and sheets of rain.

I was bombarded by worse-case-scenario fear thoughts:

You're going to end up trapped! You'll lose your newfound self-expression! What if she doesn't like it when you feel like being a couch potato? What if she falls out of love and breaks your heart? What if you fall out of love and break her heart? What if the routine of living together kills the passion? Are you going to have to get rid of a bunch of your stuff? You're going to regret this decision!! What if you move in together, you get rid of a bunch of stuff, you both fall out of love in three months, and you're stuck with a year lease, having given up your old places, which worked very well for both of you, thank you very much?! Don't say I didn't warn you!

I'm not making this stuff up. These are the actual thoughts that bombarded me as I drove that sunny day in November. And they kept bombarding me throughout the Thanksgiving holiday.

Let me be clear: they were not based in my current reality—there was nothing about this relationship or this woman that warranted such thinking. Rather, they came from all my past relationships. My body was remembering, and it was literally trying to fight off what it thought was a life-threatening situation. It reacted to the threat by activating my fight, flight, or freeze reaction: white knuckles, clenched jaw, pit in my stomach, shallow breathing, tightness in chest, heat rising up my neck.

Let me back up. My divorce after 15 years of marriage was amicable, but still traumatic and painful. After moving out of my marriage home, I began to free-fall. Everything with which I was familiar—my home, my neighborhood, my routines and rituals, my role as a husband—was stripped away. I found this to be exquisitely uncomfortable and painful.

I had the presence of mind and the support from close friends and family at the time to recognize the discomfort and to resist the urge to numb or distract myself while going through the process of separation and divorce.[3] That's another story for another time. However, it's relevant here, because I still had body and emotional memories about how disorienting and painful that process was. And right now, in this new moment of risk-taking, those memories were being activated.

I'll cut to the chase: I am writing this book from the new home, looking out over the ever-changing, breathtaking ocean view, and hearing the cry of gulls and water lapping in the background. I'm content and happy in the process of making a home with my girlfriend. I've made peace with the fear-thoughts that ran rampant through my mind, and we're experiencing the richness and fullness of a growing and expanding relationship.

But I almost didn't choose that. For a few days, I thought it was all over: short breath, tight chest, panic attack, voices in my head. It nearly derailed my vision for a better life filled with love and connection and creativity.

The thoughts bouncing around in my head were all trying to warn me of imminent danger. My sense of comfort, stability, and security were all at risk, and my thoughts were targeting anything that threatened to take those away from me.

Perhaps states of being like comfort, stability, and security aren't terribly important to you. Perhaps it's *adventure* that you long for, and anything that threatens to bring boredom is the enemy. Or perhaps it's *intimacy*, and the enemy is anything that threatens to disconnect you from your source of intimacy. Whatever it is, we all have states of being to which we are attached. Fear thoughts are triggered precisely when we are faced with circumstances that threaten these attachments—comfort, stability, security, adventure, intimacy, etc.

The Fear Reaction

And what happens when we're threatened? We fight or we flee or we freeze (or we faint). There are all kinds of ways these responses kept us alive in the caveman days. Remember the sympathetic nervous systems (SNS)? It's the SNS-activated body systems that would help us fight off the biting ants, flee from the pursuing tiger, or try to be invisible to the rattlesnake in our path. But those kinds of life-threatening circumstances and critters aren't a regular part of our lives anymore (for most of us, at least).

As it turns out, the SNS can be just as easily triggered *by our thoughts*. So, while our physical lives may not actually be threatened, our body will still respond to a story in our heads that ends in some sort of death—even the perceived or potential death of an emotional state.

Take a minute to think about your own reaction when your fears are triggered. Do you fight the perceived threat by launching into a frenzy of manic activity, maybe lashing out in anger? Do you retreat and distract yourself with busyness or substances until you're so withdrawn from life that you dull yourself to the threat? Or do you become paralyzed and hope the threat passes on its own?

My fear is an equal-opportunity employer—I'm very familiar with all these reactions. When my **fight** reaction kicks in, I go into thought-overdrive, trying to solve whatever the problem is or obsessively playing out all the possible scenarios over and over in my mind.

When my **flight** reaction engages, I numb out—searching for something, *anything*, that will envelop me and allow me several minutes, hours, or days of relief. I'm sure you're familiar with the wide range of "drugs" that can help you achieve this numbed out state: TV, trashy novels, food, alcohol, work, sex, obsessive exercise, etc. I've turned to most of these at various points in my life (except obsessive exercise—I don't really get that one, but I have friends for whom that's their numbing agent of choice).

And when my **freeze** reaction visits me, I find myself paralyzed—sometimes literally—unable to think or act in the moment. My mind completely shuts down and I can't make a decision. In extreme cases, my body freezes as my attention shrinks down—from tunnel vision into blackness.

Of course, these reactions exist on a continuum. Sometimes they're debilitating, and sometimes they're just annoying. But all the time, they cut me off from my source of freedom and limit my ability to see possibilities and act in new and healthy ways.

At this point, you may want to spend some time reflecting on your fear reactions by jotting down some thoughts or talking with someone who knows you well. See if you can describe your reaction pattern in detail. Try to identify where it starts—in your body as a feeling or in your head as a thought. It helps to understand what your particular journey down fear lane looks like because the better you know it, the more likely you are to recognize the process in its early stage. This ability to recognize your fear reaction as it's happening is important when we come to the three steps.

As a side-note, I've found a personality typology model called the Enneagram to be very helpful in my quest for greater self-awareness around my fear reaction. The Enneagram presents nine distinct personality types in terms of what each type is looking for in life and what threat each type is likely to react to (among other characteristics). It further describes different levels of reactivity for each type so that you can see what each type looks like at various points on the health scale.

What I like about the Enneagram is that it describes my default, reactive mode in such detail that I've become much more skilled at recognizing it when it's happening. Most other personality models I've worked with put you into a box. The Enneagram helps you see the box you're in so that you can climb out of it.

These are the nine basic fears represented in the Enneagram:

1. You fear losing your integrity and being corrupted.

2. You fear being unloved or unwanted by others.

3. You fear being worthless, unsuccessful, or looking bad.

4. You fear losing your sense of significance and unique identity.

5. You fear being helpless, ignorant, or inadequate.

6. You fear not having guidance or support.

7. You fear deprivation and/or pain.

8. You fear being controlled or harmed by others.

9. You fear loss and separation from others.

Do you recognize your fear in any of those statements? If so, can you put some specifics to it? When's the last time you felt this fear? How intense was it? What triggered it, and how did you react?[4]

The Fear Reaction Illustrated

Let me share another example. I think it's a helpful example because it illustrates how fear doesn't really care whether we're facing actual danger or just perceived danger. It shows what a typical fear reaction can look like as it goes from a tiny little seed of a thought to a full-blown oak tree of fight, flight, or freeze.

I've traveled a lot for my work, and getting a good seat on the plane has become both an art form and a science. If I'm not careful, it also becomes an obsession.

My ideal seat: An exit row (extra leg room) window seat (so I can see out and lean my head against the wall) with an open seat in the middle (so I can spread out and more easily make it to the aisle) with no one behind me (so I can recline without guilt) and no one in front of me (so they won't recline into my space).

Is that too much to ask?

Unfortunately for me, there's a similarly long—and unrealistic—laundry list of criteria for the perfect time of day to depart and arrive, the perfect departure city (I have a choice of three where I live), length of flight, type of aircraft, etc.

My fear is this: that I'll be stuck on a "bad" flight and be uncomfortable the whole way. I value comfort. I want to fly in comfort. I don't want to be uncomfortable. I want to sit back and disappear into the fluffy clouds, blissfully sipping a drink while watching a movie, and then drift into that hazy twilight zone state that happens at altitude (and is enhanced by alcohol at altitude).

In fairness to me, this fear—and associated desire for comfort—isn't entirely unfounded. When I was in the Navy, I had an "opportunity" to take a ride (a "hop" in Navy terms) in the back seat of an EA-6B Prowler. Important factoid: The Prowler's back seat has very little visibility of the horizon, a crucial factor in maintaining one's sense of balance.

The pilot, being the mischievous and somewhat cocky person Navy pilots tend to be, decided to see just how tough I was, starting with high-gravity turns, flipping over to negative-gravity turns, moving on to inverted turns, and finally graduating to the barrel roll.

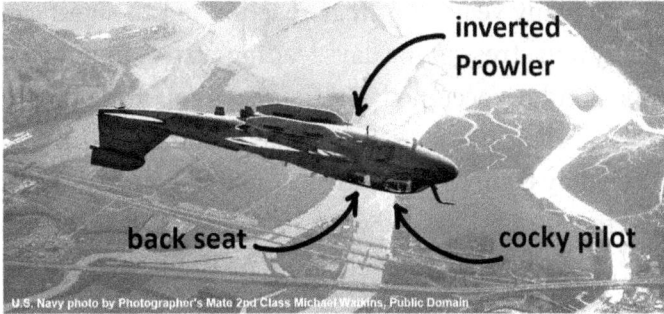

inverted Prowler

back seat

cocky pilot

U.S. Navy photo by Photographer's Mate 2nd Class Michael Watkins, Public Domain

It turns out there are three primary ways your mind tells you which way is up: vision (which visually keeps track of the horizon), your seat (which senses which way gravity is pulling you), and your inner ear (which acts kind of like a gyroscope). In my limited but potent personal experience, the barrel-roll creates a perfect storm of conflicting messages from all three of these systems. In the presence of this system overload, my body did the only thing it could do: it emptied the contents of my stomach. Quickly, violently, and repeatedly.

So, my (not completely irrational) fear kicks in the moment I start searching for a flight. Like the loyal soldier it is, my sympathetic nervous system activates as my body responds to the fear with nervous, anxious energy and shallow breathing—preparing me to fight, flee, or freeze. The thoughts that flood my mind are: *What if I'm trapped in a bad seat? What if there's turbulence and I can't find the barf bag? What if there's a better seat? What if I spend the entire flight uncomfortable and miserable?*

For many years, this fear reaction led to significant anxiety and stress in the days leading up to a flight. I was moody and preoccupied. On the morning of the flight, I awoke feeling nauseated. If I had a choice, I drove or traveled by train to avoid the whole flying ordeal. I even tried to get out of travel when I could. And If I did have to fly, I tried as hard as I could to get the perfect seat on the perfect flight.

Here's what this journey down fear lane looks like. My fear triggers an obsessive-compulsive state as I open multiple browsers so I can see all the options. My computer slows down to a crawl as each site performs its search. Picking a flight in this state can be painful, often resulting in losing the cheapest fares because I delay in the hope that I'll find a better option. When I finally decide on a flight and have to choose my seat, I second-guess myself with all kinds of psychological tricks for getting a seat that will result in no one beside me, in front of me, or behind me.

On my way to the airport, my feelings of anxiety increase as I imagine getting stuck in the security line or having to board last and not having a place for my suitcase in the overhead bin. When I take my seat, I try to look as undesirable as possible (if I'm on Southwest, where it's open seating), or I nearly stop breathing as I see if the open seat next to me will stay open as the doors close. My fight response gets triggered when it looks like I'm going to get a row all to myself, the door closes, and then someone leaves their seat and sneaks into a seat in my empty row last minute. I greet them with a forced smile and fume inside.

If I haven't dealt productively with my fear by now, it turns into resentment or discouragement as the plane takes off, thus sabotaging any hope I had of flying in comfort. What started as a fear of being uncomfortable (hearkening back to my hop in the Prowler), turns into *actual* discomfort as my thoughts run rampant and keep me from settling in, relaxing, and enjoying the ride.

This point is extremely important: **When we let our fear reaction take over, we often end up manifesting the very things we were trying so hard to avoid.**

Fear Robs Us of Health, Opportunity, and Enjoyment

This pattern of reacting to fear robs us of so much. On a physiological level, when the SNS is activated, it immediately starts to shut down non-critical body systems in order to divert precious resources to those systems that need them most when we're threatened. If we live in this state frequently enough, our bodies begin to react with increased risk of heart problems, digestive issues, ulcers, etc. It takes an emotional and psychological toll too, with potential for memory loss, difficulty making decisions, and dysregulated emotions.

But there's another price we pay. As our brains and bodies shut down to divert attention to the perceived threat, we lose sight of *possibility*. That is, we stop seeing all the options that are open to us. And all of this happens **in the very moment when we need to see options.**

When we go into our reactive fear mode, our programming kicks in, and we automatically react in ways that we've always reacted. This means that we always get the same results. Over and over and over again. The only hope we have for breaking out of our ingrained patterns is to see other options open to us and to **choose** a different path.

Perhaps the worst effect of fear is the loss of being fully present to *what is*. Reality as it unfolds in every moment is the only thing that truly exists. Everything else is merely a thought in our heads—a memory from the past or an anticipation of the future. Life is only available to us in each moment as we pass through time. And if I'm in a fear response, I'm no longer experiencing the wonderful richness and limitless depth of the see it, hear it, feel it, taste it, touch it world around me.

There's Another Way

When I've been able to disrupt my fear of air travel before the reaction happens or in the midst of it happening, I've often been surprised by what I find. I meet an interesting person in the seat next to me who happens to hold the key to the next step in my life journey. Or I engage in a genuine exchange with the check-out clerk and, in that moment, recognize that we share this profound mystery called life. Or I notice a small shop on a side street and find the perfect gift for an upcoming birthday.

The possibilities are endless when we're present to *what is* rather than being absorbed by the story playing in our heads. This is the flipside of fear.

That's why it's so important to deal with our fears. Our very lives depend on it. I mean that both literally and figuratively. The longevity of our physical lives depends on it. And the quality of our time on this earth depends on it.

Are you reaching your creative potential? Are your relationships vibrant and life-giving? Are you content and joyful? Are you surprised and delighted by the gifts life delivers every day? Are you making decisions that deliver on your dreams? If you can't answer a resounding YES! to these questions, it's time to break free. It's likely that you inherited much of your fear from your family of origin—slavery to fear is something that gets passed on from generation to generation. If you want to break the chain of fear, live a full and enriched life, and pass along that freedom to your children, *now is the time*!

CHAPTER 2

The Flipside of Fear

*Don't be afraid of your fears. They're not there
to scare you. They're there to let you know
that something is worth it.*

–C. Joybell C.

Resistance is Futile

N ow that we've explored fear and its different facets, the question begs to be asked: How do you get rid of it? The answer is simple: You don't. There it is. I've said it. You don't "get rid" of fear.

That doesn't mean, however, that fear has to be in control.

You might have heard this adage: *What you resist persists.* And so it is with fear. When you resist fear, pushing against it, it persists. I dare say, it may even grow stronger.

Unfortunately, many of us who have grown up in Western cultures have learned to resist the things we don't like. We're taught that if we try hard enough or fight hard enough, we'll break through. Think of the language we use to talk about our relationship with illness: *She's battling cancer. He's fighting a cold.* And then we have sayings like *No pain, no gain* and *What doesn't kill you only makes you stronger.*

But when it comes to fear, resistance *is* futile. Actually, resistance is like a nutrient-rich Petri dish for the fear-amoeba. The more resistance, the more the fear-amoeba grows and multiplies, grows and multiplies, grows and multiplies.

I spent most of the first half of my life perfecting the resistance approach. I pushed against fear and tried to stuff it into the back corners of my psyche where it would never be seen or heard from again.

Unfortunately, what results from this approach is neither pretty nor helpful. By pushing it down, fear becomes hard-coded into the programming of the subconscious mind. And from that hidden command post, it's able to make pronouncements and issue orders that the rest of the body believes and blindly follows. These orders are all pretty much the same:

This [undesirable situation or person] is going to cause you [some form of pain and/or death]. You need to [fight, flee, or freeze] RIGHT NOW!

What's on the Flipside?

Earlier we saw what this chain reaction can look like and where it can lead. But what's the alternative? The alternative is to find our way to the flipside of fear. Every fear has a flipside, but the flipside is usually hidden—it's on the *other* side of fear. What does that mean?

Most of the time, we only see the front side of fear— the side that activates our default reaction. We get triggered, we react, things get messy, and then we recover. And we go along our merry way naively hoping that we won't be triggered again.

It's only possible to find your way to the flipside when you're willing to approach fear and go through it. We'll explore in detail how to do that later. But what's on the flipside once you make your way there? Is the payoff worth the effort?

If fear shuts us down, closing us off to possibility and connection, the flipside is just the opposite. It turns us on and opens us up to new possibilities and ways of connecting with ourselves and others. On the flipside of fear is the pathway to breaking old patterns, to new ways of being in the world, and to infinite possibility and creativity. Sound too good to be true? Let me give you an example from a client I worked with.

Donna (not her real name) is a health care professional. In her work, she noticed how many people kept coming to her with chronic, undiagnosed health problems. In her own life, Donna had found freedom from symptoms that plagued her by changing her relationship to her illness through some regular practices and rituals based in mindfulness and awareness.

She was so profoundly impacted by her own journey of transformation that she wanted to create a workshop to help others. As we worked through the design of her workshop, she revealed a fear that plagued her: that the process she developed wouldn't work for everybody, and that when it failed, she would be humiliated and labeled a fraud.

I first asked if she would be willing to approach her fear and explore it a little. Being the courageous woman that she is, she readily agreed. So I posed this question: "What is your fear trying to protect you from?"

I encouraged her to explore her past to see if she could remember any times when she'd felt humiliated or labeled a fraud. She recounted two poignant stories: one where she felt humiliated in front of her peers due to an honest mistake and the disproportionate and harsh reaction from a colleague; and one where she felt like a fraud when a deceased patient's family members unfairly blamed her for the death.

I asked her again: What is your fear trying to protect you from?

In that moment her voice softened as she exclaimed, "It's really quite sweet. My fear is trying to keep me from feeling those things again." At that moment, Donna crossed over to the flipside of her fear.

As we tentatively took our first few steps on the flipside, Donna began to feel lighter. I asked her what might be a more inspired way to relate to her fear. She realized that, in order to help others in their healing process, she needed to make herself vulnerable. In fact, her own vulnerability would be a key ingredient in the transformation she hoped to help birth in her workshop participants.

We ended the conversation by Donna inviting her fear into a new, inspired way of being. She no longer needed protection from being vulnerable. Rather, she needed to *make herself vulnerable*, in courage and strength, to carry out her life purpose.

Donna still may feel some hesitation about this issue from time to time, but moving to the flipside has given her the courage and vision to pursue her dream of helping others through workshops. Fear of vulnerability tried to limit her, but on the flipside she found that vulnerability was the very key for offering her gift to the world.

Approaching, Accepting, and Going with the Flow

If resisting our fear leads to limits, what's the other option? Non-resistance. Non-resistance is an orientation toward adversity that is based in "going with" rather than "going against." Those who were reared in Eastern cultures are at a slight advantage here. In Eastern cultures, there seem to be more examples of non-resistance. At the risk of oversimplification: Asia gave us the martial arts, which are all about going *with* energy; Gandhi gave us a *non-violent* model for dealing with social injustice that later inspired Martin Luther King Jr. and many others; and Buddhism teaches us to accept *what is* while paying attention to the "good" and "bad" labels our mind uses. That's not to say there aren't examples of non-resistance in Western culture, but they tend to be more on the fringes. You have to go looking for them.

If resistance makes the fear-amoeba multiply and then take up residence in our subconscious programming, what happens with the non-resistance approach? Non-resistance allows us to enter into a more productive relationship with our fear by helping us sit with things as they are, rather than attacking them with a barrage of thoughts, beliefs, or knee-jerk reactions.

Our fears aren't little demons or gremlins that are intent on our destruction. Rather, each fear that we experience in the here and now came about because of a real or perceived danger at some time in the past (for example, my divorce, my traumatic flight, or Donna's painful experiences). **Our fears are trying to protect us from re-traumatization, and treating them with respect and compassion will give us significantly more desirable results than treating them with contempt or revulsion.**

There's an Opportunity Here!

If we can find a way to get a little closer to our fear, rather than pushing it down or trying to lock it in the closet, we have an opportunity. First, we have an opportunity to learn from our fear. What is it trying to protect me from and why? We also have an opportunity to invite our fear into the present, where our highest priority may no longer be avoiding danger. In fact, we have an opportunity to enlist the help of that part of us that shrinks in fear. We have an opportunity to invite it to a more inspired way of living.

Each fear has its flipside. It is this flipside that represents *freedom*. If my fear is trying to protect me from being uncomfortable on a flight, the flipside might be learning to be okay in the midst of discomfort. If my fear is trying to protect me from losing my sense of freedom by moving in with my girlfriend, the flipside might be finding a freedom that comes from within me rather than from my circumstances.

This approach doesn't mean that we give up and roll over, belly up, while fear pummels us into submission. In fact, the non-resistance approach requires great amounts of courage, presence, and inner strength. It also requires a willingness to be vulnerable, authentic, and honest with ourselves.

Introducing the Three Steps

How do you get to the flipside of fear? My psychotherapist, who helped me journey productively through my divorce uses two phrases in just about every session. The first is this: *Get spacious and curious.* I love those words—spacious and curious. They evoke light and breath and relaxation. They encourage a sort of unclenching of the fist while at the same time a slight leaning forward. And they encourage me to stand tall, look my fear in the eye, and keep breathing.

The second is this: *This is only a part of you.* This phrase invites me to see my fear differently. So instead of saying, "I'm afraid of air travel," I'd say, "A part of me is afraid of air travel." This may sound like a small, inconsequential difference. However, when I express my fear in terms of a "part of me," I'm acknowledging that I can have a relationship with fear, rather than simply being subject to fear's whims in the moment. I'm also acknowledging that there's the *rest of me*—the me that exists apart from my fear—that isn't afraid and that knows how to respond wisely.[5]

The three steps for living on the flipside of fear are based on this premise: You can get different, positive results by getting spacious and curious; awakening and engaging the part of you that is *not* your fear; and developing a positive relationship with your fear.

How do you do that? Below is a quick overview of the three steps.

Step 1: Interrupt Fear. In the moment of being triggered, interrupt the fight, flight, or freeze reaction. Find a way to activate the parasympathetic nervous system (recovery and relaxation), and introduce space between being triggered and reacting.

Step 2: Approach Fear. Once you've created some space with Step 1, get curious about your fear. Find out what belief ecosystem is operating in your mind, and explore what your fear is trying to protect you from. When you know what your fear is trying to protect you from, see if you can find compassion, empathy, and maybe even a little affection for your fear.

Step 3: Flip Fear. How would you *rather* show up in the world with respect to this fear? What's the inspired way of being? What does freedom look like? Invite your fear to the back seat as you journey to the flipside.

We'll explore each step in more detail and with examples in the next three chapters.

CHAPTER 3

Step 1: Interrupt Fear

*Your vision will become clear only when you
look into your heart. Who looks outside, dreams.
Who looks inside, awakens.*

–Carl Jung

Reacting vs. Responding

Whether it's an immediate threat or an intrusive thought, fear always begins with some sort of stimulus that triggers our fight, flight, or freeze reaction. In our unconscious, default mode, this is how the process usually plays out:

Stimulus → Reaction

We are stimulated by some sort of situation, experience, thought, etc., and immediately we react to it with our own personal version of fight, flight, or freeze. Stimulus. Reaction.

Here's an example that's familiar to me. I'm driving along in a relaxed and alert state, a car cuts me off, the driver displays the universal gesture of displeasure, and I'm immediately in a storm of thoughts ranging from anger to shame (that's the extent of my emotional range in these situations). The rest of the drive is spent going over choice words and gestures that I could have creatively and emphatically employed in the moment. The peace I might have been feeling before the incident is definitely gone.

That is what an unconscious, default mode of stimulus/reaction looks like. The key to changing this pattern is to introduce space into the equation:

Stimulus → Space → Response

Notice in this second equation I used the term "response" rather than "reaction." Reaction is the word I use for the blind, knee-jerk thing that happens when we're following our typical pattern. Response is the word I use for when we're able to *choose*. Animals react; human beings have the capacity to respond.

Introducing Space

The space in the middle of the equation is the interruption. I've found there's one thing I always have access to, and it's 100% effective at interrupting the pattern: breath. It's that simple. When we're able to breathe in the midst of fear, it's possible to move from reaction to response.

If you doubt the efficacy of breath to interrupt the fear reaction, a quick Google query will reveal extensive research that shows how deep breathing acts as a signal to the body to activate the parasympathetic nervous system, which helps us get into a more relaxed state. By mastering our breath, we're able to deactivate the SNS and activate the PNS, and this switch is all it takes to move from reacting to responding.[6]

Let's get back to the driving example. Using breath to introduce space might look like this: You're driving along in a relaxed and alert state, a car cuts you off, and the driver gives you the gesture. You notice a flash impulse to react, but before it sets in, you take a deep, conscious breath. You notice the sun, the road, the steering wheel. You breathe again, and instead of anger or shame, your mind opens to other possibilities. You might find compassion for the driver, who's so shut down that he blames you for his mistake. You recognize that he's got his own issues, and his version of reality doesn't have to be the same as yours. You keep breathing, relaxed and alert.

Building Breath Awareness

As it turns out, while it may be simple, it isn't easy. Most of us, most of the time, are completely unaware of our breath. Try this today: see if you can consciously notice your breathing pattern three times throughout the day. As you do, note the nature of the pattern. Is it shallow? Truncated? Are you holding your breath? Or are you breathing deeply and fully? When I first started paying attention to my breathing, I was surprised to notice how often I wasn't breathing at all. I was holding my breath.

Mark this page and come back to it tomorrow. When you return, ask yourself these questions:

- **Did I notice my breathing at all yesterday?**

- **If so, what was the nature of my breathing pattern?**

If the answer to the first question is "no," you're not alone. When I first tried this, it took me quite a while to actually notice my breathing. At the end of the day (or early the next day), as I remembered my intention to notice my breathing, I'd scratch my head, puzzled that once again I'd forgotten to notice.

You see, I wasn't used to stepping out of the immediate situation and simply observing what was happening in my body. That wasn't a practice or an idea I'd grown up with. It was completely foreign to me. I needed to find a way to activate this "observer" part of myself.

Meditation as a Tool

Meditation has helped me immensely. When I first tried to practice meditation, I had the misconception that the purpose was to attain some calm, Zen-like state of being. And I was constantly frustrated, because meditation simply did not have that effect on me. Just the opposite, in fact. I found myself agitated, my mind bouncing around from thought to thought.

Then I realized a different purpose for meditation: *to practice noticing.*

I began to see meditation like lifting weights. Competitive athletes who lift weights as part of their training don't do so to become better weight lifters (unless their sport is weight lifting, of course). Rather, they lift weights so that their bodies are conditioned to perform to their highest potential *in the game.*[7]

Building on the weight-lifting metaphor, I meditate so that I can better notice what's happening *in life*—as I go about my day, moment by moment. Accordingly, every time my mind wanders in meditation *and I notice that it's wandering,* I've done one repetition. The more my mind wanders in meditation, and the more I notice it, the more reps I've done. And the more I practice this, the more likely it is that I'll begin noticing what's happening in the moment in life, when all kinds of things are threatening to trigger my default, reactive patterns.

So, here's my plug for meditation: If you don't already have a daily meditation practice, I encourage you to start one today. As I've collected aids for meditation in the form of books, audio recordings, and apps, I've found two basic goals of meditation represented. The first is to practice noticing. The second is to practice generating certain kinds of thoughts and feelings. I think both are valid, but the meditation that I'm recommending here is the first: to practice noticing.

It's really quite easy. Use your phone to set a one-minute timer. And for that one minute, pay attention to your breath. You can do this while walking, sitting, lying down, looking at a candle, or doing any other activity where you can be relaxed and focused. As you focus, try paying attention to the air coming in and out of your nose, your chest rising or falling, or the air filling your belly. It doesn't matter. Pick one of those places, and pay attention. As you do, see if you can catch yourself in the moment that your mind begins to wander. That's it.

This part is very important, and it's a point that just about every mindfulness and meditation author I've read makes: When you notice that your mind is wandering (and it *will* wander), don't beat yourself up. Instead, simply say to yourself something like, "How 'bout that? My mind is wandering" and then come back to your breath. It can be kind of fun, trying to notice the very moment your mind starts to wander. The more your mind wanders (and you notice it wandering), the more reps you've done. If you're feeling brave, consider increasing your practice from one minute a day to five minutes.

This one-minute practice equipped me to begin noticing my breathing (or rather, not-breathing, in my case) throughout the day. The more I stopped to notice my breathing, the more natural it was to interrupt and approach my fear in the moment of a triggering event.

Body Awareness: Another Way to Interrupt Your Fear

There's another way to interrupt your fear: get into your body. I'm very comfortable living life above the neckline—in my mind. The problem with this is that the mind is a playground for intrusive fear thoughts. Building body awareness and directing attention to sensations in the body is another effective way to interrupt the fear reaction.

Sensation—seeing, hearing, touching, tasting, smelling—is the basis for all experience. As a living organism, we experience *everything* first through one of our five senses (some might add a sixth sense of intuition to this list). Your body, after it has registered the sensation, passes off that information to your mind. And then your mind interprets the sensation. It's that interpretation that can get us into trouble.

For example, the actual physical sensations of being excited and being frightened are very similar: you might feel a sudden jolt in your stomach followed by an adrenaline rush throughout your body. But how do you *interpret* that feeling? Excited or frightened? That's where the mind comes in. It takes that sensation, overlays a meaning, and labels it good or bad. Then you react accordingly.

Staying with the physical sensation allows you to gain some more space between the stimulus and the reaction. And sometimes that's all you need to short-circuit the chain reaction and return to a calm, non-fear state.

Noticing what's happening in your body is relatively easy. As you're reading, right now, what are you feeling? Take a moment and make a note of the sensations. For me, as I write this paragraph, I'm feeling the pressure of the seat on my bum, I'm feeling a little hungry, my eyes are feeling dry, and my body is erect and straight.

Remembering to notice what's happening in your body in the midst of a fear reaction is much harder. You can add body awareness to your meditation practice by simply noting throughout the meditation what you're feeling in your body. This will help you to stay with sensations in the moments when you are being triggered.

Interrupting your fear is a form of *waking up*. I've seen the terms "conscious," "aware," "awake," and "present" used to describe a certain state of being—when you're both participating in what's going on, but you're also aware of it. For example, I may be hearing voices in my head, and at the same time I may also be able to objectively say to myself, *you're hearing voices in your head*. In this state of being, I have a *choice* about how to respond. I'm awake.

The opposite of this state of being is when I'm "unconscious," "oblivious," "asleep" or "absent," and all I do is react to whatever is going on. And I have a whole portfolio of reactive patterns that I'm not proud of, let me tell you. Practices such as meditation and body awareness have helped me become more conscious, aware, awake, and present.[8]

From Reaction to Response

Interrupting my stimulus/reaction fear pattern with breath and body awareness has made a world of difference for me. Let me give you three examples for how these practices have moved me from my default, reactive pattern and allowed me to choose a different response. These are all situations in which my fear reaction has been triggered.

Example #1:

Stimulus: I receive criticism at work.

Fear Voice: You're not good enough. You'll never be good enough. In fact, no one really likes you.

Old, Reactive Pattern: I immediately defend myself or find fault in the other. And then my mind plays over and over even better ways of getting the upper hand.

New, Responsive Choice: I take a deep, conscious breath, look the other in the eye, and thank her for her concern and her feedback. And then I search myself for the truth in what she said, open to learning and growing.

Example #2:

Stimulus: I'm in the shower, thinking about a difficult conversation I'm planning to have with my boss.

Fear Voice: You're not going to know what to say. And if you do say something, you won't be heard.

Old, Reactive Pattern: My mind plays out all the things that I want to say to him—constant, tireless chatter in my head.

New, Responsive Choice: I take a deep, conscious breath and direct my attention to the feeling of the water on my body. I remind myself that I'll know what to say in *that* moment if I'm fully present in *this* moment.

Example #3:

Stimulus: I feel that "bump" on the plane as we're descending.

Fear Voice: This is the first bump. Turbulence will follow. Terrible turbulence. You're going to barf. And there's no barf bag.

Old, Reactive Pattern: I clench down on the hand rests, hold my breath, and tighten my belly, my eyes searching frantically for the barf bag. Then I actually start feeling sick.

New, Responsive Choice: I take a deep, conscious breath and notice how my body is reacting. I feel the seat and the armrests. I close my eyes and practice letting go and being o.k. with what is. I might even imagine I'm on a roller coaster, raising my hands in the air (not literally) and leaning into the sensation.

Interrupting a fear reaction doesn't mean that fear automatically goes away. Rather, it gives me a way through it—a way to introduce space before my reaction kicks in. I immediately feel more present, more grounded, more connected to myself and to others. The fear feels less active. **And I can choose how to respond.** It's good. And it sets a solid foundation for Step 2.

Put it into Practice!

- **Do:** Schedule a one-minute meditation for yourself at the same time every day.

- **Do and Reflect:** Set an intention to notice your breathing three times throughout the day. Come back to it the next day and reflect on your experience.

- **Reflect:** What fear shows up in your life regularly that you'd like to use as you explore this process? Pick one and keep it in mind as you read further.

CHAPTER 4

Step 2: Approach Fear

What you fear is an indication of what you seek.
–Thomas Merton

Exploring and Making Peace

With the space opened up by Step 1, it's now time to approach your fear. You can take this step either in the midst of the fear—as it's happening—or when you're removed from the source of fear. The point of Step 2 is to explore and to make peace with your fear. At the end of this step, you'll better understand your fear, you'll have some empathy and compassion for it, and you'll have a springboard for finding the flipside.

Approaching your fear starts with some exploration questions.

Exploration Question 1: What are My Thoughts?

What are my thoughts? brings us above the neck-line, to our mind. If you hadn't first created some space in Step 1, the thoughts in your mind would exist at the subconscious level, and you'd believe them without question. But with some space, you can view your thoughts like you might view sky-writing or a movie screen. *You have* your thoughts rather than your thoughts *have you*, and you can observe them without grabbing onto them.

What does the sky-writing say? My sky-writing al-most always starts with some form of "What if?" This is my fear's favorite tool for derailing me. I *what-if* myself into paralysis and inaction. Let's go back to my big deci-sion to move in with my girlfriend. To remind you, these are the thoughts that made their way across my mind-scape as I was curled up in my fetal fear position:

> *You're going to end up trapped! You'll lose your newfound self-expression! What if she doesn't like it when you feel like being a couch potato? What if she falls out of love and breaks your heart? What if you fall out of love and break her heart? What if the routine of living together kills the passion? Are you going to have to get rid of a bunch of your stuff? You're going to regret this decision!! What if you move in together, you get rid of a bunch of stuff, you both fall out of love in three months, and you're stuck with a year lease, having given up*

your old places, which worked very well for both of you, thank you very much?! Don't say I didn't warn you!

Your fear thoughts—your mental sky-writing—may look slightly different. For example: *You'll just end up [fill in the blank]!* or *Who do you think you are??* In her book, *Big Magic*, Elizabeth Gilbert points out that every fear can be simplified to this one, basic command: Stop it. She cites fear as the number one source of creative block and that thing which prevents us from living to our potential. I agree. Regardless of the details of your fear thoughts, they all have the same implicit message: DON'T DO IT.

Exploring your fear thoughts brings them into the light where you can begin to relate to them differently. When your fear thoughts stay in the dark—in your subconscious programming—you react to them automatically, without question. Bringing them out into the open allows your conscious mind to see them for what they are.

And what are they? Fear thoughts are the visible tip of a much larger iceberg (or what I like to call a "fearberg"). What's below the waterline is the belief ecosystem—the story—that contains the *reason why* your fear keeps showing up.

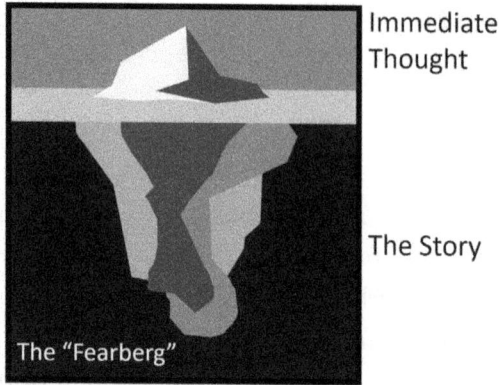

Immediate Thought

The Story

The "Fearberg"

Exploration Question 2: What's the Story?

What's the story? gets us to the heart of the matter. Using my flying example, an immediate thought might be: *Uh-oh, I'm going to be uncomfortable on the plane.* This thought kicks up the fear of being uncomfortable and trapped. Left unchecked, it results in the chain reaction I described earlier.

But that thought doesn't exist independently. It's supported by a whole story. The belief ecosystem, or story, behind that thought might be this: *Discomfort is the enemy. It must be avoided at all costs. I was extremely uncomfortable once, and I never want to go there again. Only bad things come from discomfort.*

As I've explored the stories behind my own fears, I've noticed that every fear is about the fear of death—the death of whatever emotional state I'm attached to. Death looks different for each fear, but it all boils down to fear trying to protect me from its particular form of death: for example, the death of comfort, the death of freedom, the

death of self-expression. Once realized, this understanding opens up a whole new possibility: **Your fear has
been trying to protect you. It's been trying to help
you, not harm you.** And this makes all the difference.

Fear as an Ally?

It's worth pausing in the process here and contem-
plating this new possibility—your fear is actually your
ally. If you're like me, you've seen fear as the enemy—as
President Franklin Roosevelt said, "The only thing we
have to fear is fear itself." The notion that fear is an ally
feels very wrong at first. But when you uncover the reason for your fear—the way your fear has been trying to
protect you—then you begin to see things a little differently, and that opens up a world of new possibilities.

Let's go back to my flying example. My fear remembers how uncomfortable and terrifying it was for my 20-
year old self to be strapped into the back seat of that jet,
oxygen mask constricting my breathing, as my world
spun around me and my body reacted with nausea and
vomiting.

There's an interesting side note here. I didn't feel this
fear when I donned the flight suit and climbed up the
ladder into the Prowler. I was excited as I anticipated the
experience of hurtling through the air strapped to a
rocket. I knew it was possible, and even likely, that I
would toss my cookies, so I placed barf bags strategically
around my flight suit for easy access. It wasn't until I actually had the uncomfortable experience that my fear

kicked in. My fear remembers what it felt like in my body to feel confined, trapped, and sick in the back seat of the Prowler, and from that point on, it's been on a mission to protect me from ever experiencing those sensations again. Here's the reason for this fear's existence:

My fear is trying to protect me from ever feeling trapped, helpless, and uncomfortable again.

Said this way, I can start to have some compassion for my fear. In fact, when I see my fear as an ally, it opens up the possibility that I can even enlist its help. Perhaps I can explain to my fear that there's a better way to help than fighting, fleeing, or freezing. We'll get to that in Step 3.

In this new space, I begin to soften. For the first time, I catch a glimpse that all along my fear has been trying to help me. I might be a little surprised by this realization, or I might find a bit of compassion. I've now seen my fear in a way that I haven't ever seen it before. Where before I tried to avoid my fear, now I approach it, listen to it, see it. And *being heard and seen* disarms the fear. Fear is no longer the enemy, and I can begin to approach it even more.

Naming Your Fear

Fear is such a serious thing. When we talk about being afraid, we get all furrow-browed and pursed-lips. What would it look like if we could loosen up a little bit? Naming your fear brings a little levity to the matter.

But it does more than that. As adults, we typically give nicknames to the people or animals we're fond of. It communicates a kind of sweet affection to the object of the nickname. I had at least 50 nicknames for my sweet little toy Poodle. Max was my spirit animal—that rare find of an animal who's put into your life to teach you how to live more fully and be more you. Some of his nicknames were permanent and oft-used—Chicken Bear, Mouse Bear, Fuzzy Beast, Fuzzy Rumpkin, Phroggy. Other nicknames were situational and used only once or twice. I like to think he felt my affection and acceptance each time I called him by a nickname.

And that's what we're going for here: a sort of affection for and acceptance of our fear. Knowing how our fear has been trying to protect us, we can offer it a nickname that makes it part of the gang.

I've named my fear of being uncomfortable on a plane *Neurotic Nellie*. Neurotic Nellie is constantly on the lookout for things that will cause me discomfort, and when she sees something, she speaks up.

By naming a fear, you have a sort of short-hand way of referring to everything about that fear. You can dialogue with it—*Ah, there you are again, Neurotic Nellie. Don't worry, we'll be just fine on this flight.*

Our fears tend to want to lurk in the dark corners of our mind, loathe to come out into the light, not wanting to be exposed. Naming Neurotic Nellie has helped coax her into the light and keep her there.

For another example, let's go back to my decision to move in with my girlfriend. Backing up a bit, when I set up my post-divorce bachelor pad, I discovered my adult sense of style. I hadn't lived alone since I was in my 20s, and decorating my home in my 40s gave me a chance to explore and express myself aesthetically as a mature adult.

At first, I bought functional furniture off Craigslist or at yard sales just to fill the space with the things I needed. After some time, I made some larger purchases—a dining room table, a new couch, a big living room rug, some original art. I'd never made that kind of investment in my own, individual sense of style. I realized that my space and how I decorate and arrange it matter to me and have a huge impact on my mood. I learned that I have a style and I like to express it.

Now, as I was setting up home with my girlfriend, who also has a strong sense of style (and had her own complete set of furnishings and art), I was feeling fear show up with voices like:

You're giving up your ability to express yourself!

Do you really like that, or are you just going along with it to keep the peace?

You're getting rid of what?? But you searched so long and hard for that!

Sell the couch and you're selling a little piece of your soul. You'll never get that back!

At first, these voices were extremely confusing and disconcerting. In fact, shortly after we moved in, I found myself laying on her couch in the living room (my couch was disassembled in the corner in the to-be-sold pile) suffering shortness of breath and tightness in my chest as the voices bombarded me—all the signs of a mild panic attack. The voices culminated in this fear-based belief: *Every piece you give away is a piece of your identity, your soul.*

Over the following days, I explored this fear more deeply, and what I saw was a fear who was trying to protect me from losing my voice and my connection to myself. He was trying to protect the hard-won sense of self-expression that I'd found while setting up my bachelor pad. As I played with different names to give this fear, *The Artiste* seemed fitting.

The Artiste is shorthand for this jumble of voices and thoughts. By naming this fear, my relationship with it is more visible, more conscious. And rather than being banned to the dark corners of my mind, The Artiste now has an open invitation to join the gang. I understand that The Artiste has just wanted to be seen and heard, and my nickname communicates my acceptance of and affection for this part of me.

Steps 1 and 2 Illustrated

Let's summarize what we've learned and see what Steps 1 and 2 look like in practice. Where we left off with the moving-in-with-my-girlfriend story was that my fear thoughts were showing up full force as I was driving to Pennsylvania on that sunny November day.

In the moment of bombardment, I engaged in Step 1: Interrupt Fear. I began taking slow, conscious breaths as I was driving. I deactivated my SNS (fight, flight, or freeze) and activated my PNS (recovery and relaxation), telling my body that there was no immediate danger. And I opened my senses to what I was feeling in my body: fingers squeezing the steering wheel. Knuckles white. Breathing very shallow, and at times not breathing at all. Clenching teeth, tight jaw. Heat rising up my neck. Pit in my stomach. Tightness in my chest. I also opened up my senses to the world around me: blue sky with lazy clouds, trees passing by, other cars, the road.

More breathing. More sensing.

While driving, I called a friend and asked for help remembering what I knew to be true about myself, my girlfriend, and my decision to move in with her. I didn't spend a lot of time describing my fears—they didn't need more air time at this point. Rather, I tried to interrupt the fear barrage with thoughts and beliefs that I knew were true, but that I was having difficulty remembering in this moment of panic.

A couple days later, when I was sipping morning coffee with my sister at her house, I entered into Step 2: Approach Fear. As it turns out, each of the thoughts that I identified was generated by a unique fear, and each had its own story. As I explored the story for each fear, I discovered what each one was trying to protect me from.

The first fear in the line-up was represented by this thought:

Fear Thought: *You're going to end up trapped!*

I asked myself what the story behind this thought was and narrated it from the voice of my fear (being as over-the-top and dramatic as I could):

> **Fear's Story:** *I fought hard to help you become independent and free after your divorce. Moving in with your girlfriend is going to set you back. Way back. Say goodbye to freedom, dude! You're going to end up trapped—unable to make your own decisions, decorate your home the way you want, eat whatever you want, go wherever and whenever you want. You will be a prisoner. Don't say I didn't warn you!*

Do you notice how writing this from the perspective of fear—as if the voice of fear is speaking to you—starts to introduce some objectivity? You are not your fear. Fear is only a part of you, and you can begin to dialogue with it. This differentiation is critical for being able to move through the process. If you can't find this healthy distance from your fear—this objectivity—it will be hard to move any further. Your fear will remain firmly entrenched in its subconscious command post.

Fear's story revealed the purpose for my fear.

Fear's Purpose: *My fear is trying to protect me from losing my newfound sense of freedom. It feels threatened by this new situation and wants to run back to the solitude and freedom of the bachelor pad.*

Now I'm back in my non-fear first-person voice. This question is activating that part of me that isn't fearful. It's also activating my empathy as I try to see things from the perspective of my fear. This orientation of empathy totally disarms and deactivates the part of me that wants to fight, flee, or freeze.

I continued this process for each of my fears that showed up during the move-in process. Here's what I discovered:

- **The Freedom Fighter** was trying to protect me from becoming trapped and stifled.

- **The Couch Potato** was trying to protect my sense of agency—the ability to do what I want when I want to do it, even if it means being a couch potato.

- **The Artiste** was trying to protect my sense of self expression.

- **The Peacemaker** was trying to protect me from the discomfort of conflict.

- **The Casanova** was trying to protect me from committing to the "wrong" person.

- **The Passionista** was trying to protect me from settling for mediocrity and losing my passion for life.

- **The Hoarder** was trying to protect me from ever being caught without something I need.

- **The Caretaker** was trying to protect me from sacrificing my needs and voice.

- **The Spiritual Drill Sergeant** was trying to protect me from becoming complacent and lazy in my quest for spiritual growth. The Spiritual Drill Sergeant saw it as his role to manage the rest of the members of the gang.

Each of these fears, when it acted up, fired off a barrage of voices in my head and sensations in my body that signaled all was not right. But they were operating on past information—stories and body memories from times I've been burned. All was well (and *is* well!), and going through Steps 1 and 2 helped me realize this more clearly and live into it.

Making Peace

At this point in the process, you might be experiencing some unfamiliar feelings for your fear—appreciation, gratitude, empathy. Discovering what it was that your fear was trying to protect you from opens up a new space within. You really can't blame your fear for trying to protect you. As far as it knows, there's a life-threatening situation out there.

When we're able to approach our fear, setting aside our usual trepidation or aversion, we see that all along our fear has had good intentions. In fact, our fear is a necessary part of a whole, healthy, and productive life. In this final part of Step 2, it's time to give your fear something that it's probably never before experienced: thanks and appreciation.

Here's a script I've found to be helpful:

> *[Fear Nickname], I understand that all along you've been trying to protect me from [fill in the blank]. Thank you for trying to keep me from harm. There's no danger here. You can relax now.*

This act of making peace with your fear opens the door wide to its flipside. Your fear has been seen, heard, understood, and appreciated. This is all it's ever wanted, and now it can step out of the way. It can now leave behind its attention-getting tactics and get into the back seat of the car. Whenever you recognize it starting to act up again, just repeat the script:

> *I see you, [Fear Nickname]. Thank you for trying to protect me. There's no danger here. You can relax now.*

In the next chapter, we'll explore the final step in the process—flipping your fear into a vision for how you'd rather live.

Put it into Practice!

Using one fear that you've identified:

- **Reflect:** What thoughts do you have when that fear comes up?

- **Reflect:** What's the story? What kind of "death" is your fear trying to protect you from?

- **Do:** Give your fear a nickname.

- **Do:** Write out a dialogue with your fear in your journal.

- **Do:** Make a name tag for your fear. Embellish it with color and art. Give it a sense of style appropriate for that fear.

- **Do:** Thank your fear and honor it for trying to protect you. Do this in writing and do it out loud. If you want to go one step further, ask a close friend to serve as a proxy for your fear and put on the nametag. Speak your thanks to your friend while looking him or her in the eye.

CHAPTER 5

Step 3: Flip Fear

*Courage is the ability of letting go of
something that makes you comfortable for
something that makes you happy.*

–Luis D. Ortiz

When Your Operating System Needs an Upgrade

We've talked about our default mode—that old familiar pattern that kicks in whenever a particular fear is triggered. This can be compared to a computer's operating system. As long as the operating system supports the programming, it will run without a hitch every time, over and over again. Problems arise when you try to run more and more complex programs on an outdated operating system.

When I was fresh out of college at my first job in the Navy, managing construction contracts on the Navy base in Guantanamo Bay, Cuba, Microsoft released Windows 95. I remember how the new operating system looked so different, so fresh. Sure, there was a learning curve, but it felt like the new operating system made everything run smoother and faster.

And it did. Until newer versions of Word and Power-Point and Quicken and all the other programs I used were released. They were optimized to run on the new Windows operating system each time Microsoft up-graded—Windows 98, and then Windows 2000, and then Windows XP, etc.

But Windows 95 was so comfortable! I didn't want to upgrade to a new operating system. For a while, I was able to string along my computer. But before long, I was all too often drumming my fingers, waiting for a pro-gram or operation to execute. Finger-drumming went to head-banging, and nearly to keyboard smashing. It be-came increasingly frustrating to operate Windows 95 when all the programs I used required more processing power than my computer had.

Our fear is similar. It's like an operating system that governs what kinds of experiences we're able to take in and process. There may have been a time when that op-erating system worked just fine. But as we grow and ma-ture in life, we start to take on more and more. Life re-quires us to run bigger and more complex programs. Sometimes we're unable to take in this new complexity in a productive way, because our fear operating system gets gummed up. It can't handle it. When this happens, we build all kinds of protections—firewalls and anti-virus programs—to keep out anything that threatens the status quo.

As I approached the decision to make my big move, I found myself face-to-face with the limitations of my operating system. Since my divorce, my operating system had become highly tuned for a certain kind of life—single, free, comfortable, secure, etc. But what would happen when I threw new conditions at it? Would it survive?

Well, if I listened to my fear voice, the answer was clear: *Absolutely NOT! Death, despair, destruction!*

One day, while reflecting on this from the comfort of my bachelor pad, I decided to make two lists of words. The first was words associated with a decision to stay, and the second was words associated with a decision to go.

Here are the two lists:

Stay Words: Comfort, Stability, Familiar, Known, Routine, Peace, Safe, Relief, Regret, Numb, Muffled, Relaxed, Settled, Status quo

Go Words: Adventure, Yes!, Flow, Courage, Energetic, New, Change, Uplifting, Community, Purpose, Calling, Relationship, Fresh, Quiet, Calm, Peace, Expansion, Connection, Alive, Vibrant

What do you notice about these two lists? Here are some of my observations:

- The Go list is longer.

- "Peace" is on both lists. (It's interesting that both the Go and the Stay decision might result in some form of peace.)

- The Stay list has more words that I would classify as "negative," but they're not all negative. (In fact, I tried to keep both lists as positive as I could in order to compare apples to apples.)

As I reflected on these two lists, I noticed something perhaps more important than the actual words. I noticed what was happening inside of me. The Stay list gave me a feeling of constriction, closing down. And the Go list gave me a feeling of opening up. There were many words on the Stay list that I was attached to—comfort, stability, familiar, routine, safe. And the prospect of making a decision that pulled those things out from under me activated my fear, even as I was drawn to the words on the Go list. I was ready for an operating system upgrade. But how to do that?

What Does the Flipside Look Like?

By this time, having gone through the first two steps, I knew how to treat fear when it showed up. I breathed deeply and greeted fear by name: *Hello Freedom Fighter, I see you. Thank you for trying to protect me. There's no danger here. Hey there, Couch Potato. I see you. Thank you for trying to protect me. There's no danger here.*

As I reflected further on the Go list, I recognized that my inspired self, that part of me that wasn't controlled by fear, wanted the things on *that* list—adventure, flow, community, purpose, expansion, alive, vibrant.

And in that moment, I realized something very important: If I oriented myself around protecting the things on the first list, **I would choose to avoid anything that challenged them until my last, dying breath.**

When I came to this realization, it was life-changing and profound. I began to reflect back on my life, marking the decisions I'd made along the way that led to a bigger life, a more complete me—growth and expansion. I was no stranger to this process. **What was noteworthy about each life decision that came to mind was how it was always accompanied by the fear of the unknown.**

There was the time I decided to study abroad in Germany my junior year in college. And then when I made a commitment to serve in the Navy. Each tour of duty that I chose in the Navy came with a vast set of unknowns and risks. Deciding to go back to school for my master's degree. Deciding to marry. Deciding to try to have children. Deciding to not have children after two miscarriages. Deciding to divorce. Deciding to leave my full-time job to strike off on my own, etc.

I'd done this before! And each time I did, I experienced the same pattern:

1. A new opportunity presents itself.

THE FLIPSIDE OF FEAR

2. I'm inspired by the new possibilities.

3. I experience some resistance and fear as I contemplate letting go of the old.

4. I make a decision to Go.

5. In that space between decision and action, fear assaults me again.

6. I push through and enter into the new experience.

7. My life expands beyond what I could have imagined.

When I move through the fear, my life always expands beyond what I could have imagined. What I was experiencing during my move-in process was that onslaught of fear as I contemplated letting go of the old. What I needed to do was connect to the possibilities of the new.

The Gift of Fear: An Inspired Life

And this right here is the gift of fear: **Your fear is the flag, the barometer, that indicates the potential for growth and expansion that's opened up in front of you.** When fear kicks in, you are at the threshold of a new experience that's been placed in your path for your evolution in this life journey. And to the extent that fear shows up in force, to that same extent, you can expect growth if you choose to face it. Small fear? Small growth. Big fear? Big growth.

What does this growth look like? This is what I call *the flipside*. This is the upgraded operating system so you can run all those cool, new programs and fly through all the processing tasks that gummed up the old system. This is *inspired living*!

Step 3 is about articulating the flipside in terms that your fear can understand. In the previous steps, you identified the ways that your fear has been trying to protect you. Step 3 is about taking off the chains, imagining, and actuating an inspired life beyond the fear.

Let me give you an example. In the previous steps, one of the fears I identified was The Freedom Fighter. In exploring this fear, I discovered that The Freedom Fighter was trying to protect my newfound freedom and independence. He was trying to prevent me from feeling trapped and stifled by preserving the living arrangements that had brought about this newfound freedom: for example, living alone, being able to make all my own decisions, not having someone at home to whom I was accountable. He had what he thought were my best interests in mind.

But I'd learned a lot about freedom in the past few years. The kind of freedom that The Freedom Fighter was familiar with was the lowest kind of freedom—freedom *from* responsibility and constraint. That kind of freedom felt really great, but I'd learned there was a price to pay. To maintain this "circumstantial freedom," I had to give up the very things I found to be life-giving—community, relationship, love, purpose, and interdependence.

In my journey away from climbing the corporate ladder in the traditional work world, I ran into books and online videos by people (mostly men in their 20s) trying to sell a kind of care-free lifestyle—work a few hours a week and live on a beach in Bali, doing whatever you please whenever you please. And I even tried out this kind of lifestyle for a time. What I learned was that leisure for leisure's sake was not something worth living for. A life of leisure with total and complete freedom from interdependent relationships or accountability to others was a numbing, colorless, dead existence for me.

And yet . . . a part of me REALLY WANTED that. I felt the lure of it, the tug, even as I was clear that it wasn't life-giving. It wasn't *inspired living*.

Simultaneously, I'd been discovering another kind of freedom that wasn't based on external circumstances. This was a freedom cultivated inside me—a freedom of thought and spirit that emanated from me when I was living well. I could experience this kind of freedom just as easily when I was up against a deadline at work or choosing how to spend time with my girlfriend.

This freedom wasn't something that I needed to protect and guard. Rather, this freedom was something that I could cultivate inside of me and give to those around me as a gift. My true condition (and your true condition) is one of freedom. I *am free*. And with this intrinsic freedom, I could free those around me from having to act or be a certain way to make me happy.

This was a freedom experienced within the context of responsibility and constraint. This was a freedom that would allow me to live a more purposeful and inspired life, entering into commitments and making promises to the world that I fully intended to keep. And *that's* how I wanted to live from now on! That was my inspired way. As often happens, I was helped in this awareness by a wise teacher. David Deida and his writings about masculinity and freedom helped me to articulate the flipside of The Freedom Fighter.[9]

I went through this same process with all my fears associated with the big move—I identified the flipside, the path I was being called to take. Here they are:

The Freedom Fighter.

> **This Fear's Intention**: You're trying to protect my newfound sense of freedom and independence.

> **This Fear's Flipside**: I'm ready to discover a new kind of freedom that comes from within me and isn't dependent on external circumstances.

The Artiste.

> **This Fear's Intention**: You're trying to help protect my voice and sense of self expression.

> **This Fear's Flipside**: I'm ready to stay connected to myself in the context of relationship and express my likes/dislikes alongside someone else's.

The Caretaker.

>**This Fear's Intention**: You're trying to keep me from losing myself in the needs of another—trying to manage my emotions through the emotions of another.

>**This Fear's Flipside**: I have a new source of well-being that comes from inside me and is not dependent on another's emotional state.

The Couch Potato.

>**This Fear's Intention**: You're trying to protect my ability to do what I want when I want, free from the expectations of another.

>**This Fear's Flipside**: I'm ready to use my downtime a little more creatively. Being a couch potato has its place, but I want to balance that with ways that bring my gifts to the world and recharge me at the same time.

The Heartbreaker.

>**This Fear's Intention**: You're trying to protect me from the relationship ending and one or both of us getting our heart broken.

>**This Fear's Flipside**: Regardless of where this relationship goes, love is worth investing in. *Love* lasts forever. I'm ready to take the risk of living

open-heartedly, loving now, in this moment, without regard for the future.

The Casanova.

This Fear's Intention: You're trying to protect me from closing down all my options and committing to the "wrong" person.

This Fear's Flipside: There is no such thing as the wrong person. I'm ready to say yes to this one woman, knowing that my focus is soil from which intimacy and vulnerability can grow.

The Passionista.

This Fear's Intention: You're trying to protect me from falling back into a non-feeling, numbed-out existence.

This Fear's Flipside: I'm ready to risk living with an open heart, cultivating and maintaining my connection to self, which is my source of passion.

The People Pleaser.

This Fear's Intention: You're trying to protect me from conflict and the negative feelings of others.

This Fear's Flipside: I'm ready to get my sense of well-being from my own inner source. I'm ready to simply *be me*. And this authenticity will enrich my connection with others.

These were some of the fears that were associated with my decision to move. When I actually moved, and we were going through the process of merging two households, a couple more fears showed up in force:

The Hoarder.

> **This Fear's Intention**: You're trying to protect me from ever being without something that I need.

> **This Fear's Flipside**: I'm ready to let go of everything that doesn't serve me *right now*. I trust that what I need will come to me when I need it.

The Sentimentalist.

> **This Fear's Intention**: You're trying to protect me from losing my connection to my past by never letting go of stuff with sentimental value.

> **This Fear's Flipside**: I'm ready to create a space that has in it only those things that serve me and match my energy *now*. Everything from my past that matters is already a part of me—I don't need to cling to stuff.

Each of these fears has its own belief ecosystem. It's an ecosystem based in limits and lack. That's what keeps us from living an inspired life and reaching our potential. Step 3 is a powerful step for making this ecosystem explicit—taking it out from under the shadows and examining it. As you do so, you can't help but ask yourself: *Do I want to continue to believe this? Does it serve me?*

Is there a more inspired way of living life? What might that look like?

How Do You Find the Flipside?

As you go through the steps, when you come to the point of identifying the flipside, it may just come to you in a flash—*Yes! This is the way I want to be living!* If it doesn't, here's a process for identifying the flipside.

Once you've figured out what your fear has been trying to protect you from, write it down. Let's use The Caretaker as an example:

You're trying to keep me from losing myself in the needs of another—trying to manage my emotions through the emotions of another.

Now, with that statement in front of you, come up with beliefs that lie behind the statement. For example:

- The other person's needs are more important than mine.

- I can only be happy if the other person is happy.

- My emotional reality is dependent on the other person's emotional state.

Examine each of those beliefs in light of what you know *at this point in your life* to be true. Write down those new beliefs. For example:

- My needs are important. I can only help another person meet her needs if I'm meeting mine, too.

- Happiness is an inside job. My happiness is my responsibility.

- The other person is free to have her emotional reality. It doesn't have to affect me. I'm the only one responsible for my emotional reality.

Armed with these new beliefs, you can articulate the flipside. For example:

- I have a new source of well-being now—it comes from inside me, and it's not dependent on another's emotional state.

Once you've written down the flipside, ask yourself: *Is this really how I want to live?* Pay attention to how your body responds. Does it feel lighter? Do you lean forward? Do you sit up straight? Or do you slouch and collapse? **Your body will tell you whether you've identified the flipside or whether you're still being limited by fear.**

There are likely as many ways to find the flipside as there are different kinds of personalities. If writing doesn't work for you, try something else. Here are some more ideas:

- Draw or paint the flipside.

- Dance the flipside.

- Visualize the flipside.

- Come up with a color that represents the flipside and find ways to surround yourself with that color.

- Talk about the flipside with another person.

- Write a poem that describes the flipside.

- Find an exercise or sport that gets your blood pumping while considering the flipside.

- Find music that represents the flipside and listen to it over and over.

- Take a walk in nature as you reflect on the flipside.

- Ask your pet to help you find the flipside and then spend some time playing with him or her.

- Pray and ask God to help you find the flipside.

- Watch a movie or read a book with characters you admire, and as you do, ask yourself how they might reveal the flipside.

If the flipside doesn't come to you the first time you contemplate it, don't worry. It often takes several iterations for us to discern what our intuition is telling us. Engaging in activities that you find inspiring can help you strengthen the connection to your intuition.

Bottom line: the flipside will occur to you when you're feeling GOOD. So, do what feels good—cook, nap, exercise, be with friends, pet your dog, cat, or fish—as you're in the process of finding the flipside.

Put it into Practice!

- **Reflect:** What might the flipside look like for the fear you're exploring?

- **Do:** Write down the flipside. To discover the flipside, use one of the methods discussed in this chapter, or come up with your own.

- **Do:** Do something this week that simply feels good. As you do, pause and notice how good it feels. Take it in.

CHAPTER 6

Living on the Flipside of Fear

What is your biggest fear? . . .
I'm afraid that I'll die without having lived fully. . . .
I'm afraid that I may be missing some magnificent
possibility. That perhaps I have not risked enough to
find it. That maybe I've lived too safe a life.

–Stephen Cope

Old Fears

In my experience, when you go through the three steps, there's immediate relief that comes with each step. However, the greater benefit is that by going through the steps, you're building muscle memory. And that muscle memory will kick in the next time the fear shows up. What's contained in your muscle memory? If you've done the three steps, this is what you've been practicing:

- Building space between stimulus and reaction, where you have time to choose how you want to respond.

- Getting curious and identifying the belief eco-system and self-limiting stories behind each fear, which yield rich insight into how your fear has been trying to protect you. This also points the way to the flipside.

- Approaching your fear from a place of gratitude and empathy, with non-resistance, which deac-tivates your fear's need to get your attention and invites it to join the gang.

- Seeing and tapping into new, inspired ways of living, full of passion, purpose, and love.

Once you've gone through the three steps with a given fear, that doesn't mean it will never show up again. The difference now is that you have a way of channeling the fear-energy into something much more productive.

Over time, old fears will begin to lose their power. What at first felt like a big, scary, overwhelming jumble of anxious thoughts and emotions might eventually begin to feel like an annoying little fly. Yes, old fears can keep showing up, but once they've been seen, recog-nized, and honored for what they were trying to protect you from (and point you *toward*), their attention-getting tactics will become less and less disturbing.

There may be times when a new experience or situation will trigger an old fear in a new or deeper way. Far from being something to be distressed about, this new dimension of the old fear carries with it a corresponding new dimension to the flipside. It gives insight into the next step in your journey toward freedom, growth, expansion, passion, purpose, and love.

When the fears I've written about first showed up, they were overwhelming. They induced mild panic attacks, and they nearly derailed my vision of entering into a deeper relationship. I still see them show up around my new home, as I continue to adjust to the new routines and ways of living needed for sharing space with an intimate partner. But now I can smile and wave at them as they cruise by in whatever form they choose to appear that day.

And I'm also grateful for them. The Freedom Fighter helped me discover a deeper and more fulfilling way to be free—a way that's always available to me and not dependent on circumstances. The Artiste has shown me that co-creation is a whole other way of bringing beauty into the world that I never could have done alone. And The Caretaker has helped me uncover the importance of dancing to the beat of my own drum, finding my sense of emotional well-being from inside of me rather than from someone else's emotional state or perceived approval of me. I could describe similar, inspired ways of being associated with each of my fears.

These ways of being are the flipside of fear. This is the inspired life that I may never have found had my fears not alerted me and pointed me in the right direction. However, living into that vision of an inspired life doesn't just come automatically.

New Fears

Because we're humans limited to time and space, and because we live in a world full of diversity, we will continue to encounter situations and people who trigger us. New fears will show up. This isn't a sign that you've lost ground or back-slipped. No, this is just a sign that you're a living, breathing human being. The more fears you take through the three steps, the more readily you'll be able to recognize the little footprints of a new fear as it makes its way through your mind.

I believe there are at least two types of new fear. The first type of new fear isn't really new. It just feels that way. It's a fear that's been operating in the background all along, but you just hadn't recognized it, yet. Remember, we all have a well-developed belief ecosystem and an elaborate reaction pattern around real or perceived threats. That belief ecosystem has been operating in your subconscious. And you have developed protective habits that kick in automatically when triggered.

There comes a time, however, when you catch a first glimpse of these reactive patterns. The more developed your daily practice of mindfulness and paying attention is, the more quickly you'll recognize the signs that a fear is emerging. Pay attention to these moments—they're gifts.

Recognition of a new fear usually happens at the intuitive level first. You sense that there's more to your thoughts and actions than what you're consciously aware of. You may get an uncanny feeling that someone else is running the show. You begin to see the patterns—*Wow, I always [fill in the blank] when [fill in the blank] happens.* If you're fortunate enough to have honest friends or family, they may help open your eyes to the ways you're habitually reacting.

When these moments happen, *don't turn away*. Make a choice to stay present to what your intuition is trying to show you. Interrupt it and approach it. Breathe. If you do, your fear will slowly reveal itself, like a groundhog tentatively emerging from its hole.

You can begin the three steps at this moment of recognition. It might feel like you're not making much progress at first—lots of stops and starts. That's normal. It takes practice to coax your fear out into the open while maintaining awareness and preventing yourself from going into fight, flight, or freeze.

Keep at it. Be diligent about interrupting your fear reactions, and approach your fear with curiosity and understanding—get spacious and curious. As you do, you'll find your fear take on form and personality, and the belief ecosystem and story behind your fear will emerge. By the time you're ready to give your fear a nickname, you'll probably already have one at the ready. You can't help but find the flipside from this place of knowledge, compassion, and openness.

The other type of new fear is a fear that's in the process of being formed. This usually happens when we do something with an open heart and end up getting hurt. We look back on these experiences and marvel at how ignorant we were. This feeling of being burned, of being naïve enough to have trusted someone or to have tried out a new experience, is a sure sign that a new fear is incubating. Once the fear is birthed, it starts running the show, and we do everything we can to avoid being hurt in the same way ever again.

Allow me to illustrate. I don't like boats. Or, more specifically, I don't like being in a boat in open, turbulent water. And even more specifically, I don't like being seasick. When people learn this about me, they point out the irony that I was in the Navy. Let me set the record straight: other than my days in training as a Navy Midshipman, I never went out on those big, gray floaty things. I was a dirt sailor. I managed construction projects in the Navy's Civil Engineer Corps and Seabees. When we deployed, we did so on planes to shore-based installations.

Where did this fear of being seasick come from? I was a junior in high school living in Bonn, Germany. My church youth group was taking a trip to a gathering in England and had to cross the English Channel on a ferry to get there. *How cool, I get to cross the English Channel on a big boat!*

And it was cool, at first. But as night fell, so did the sky. A storm hit us, and all throughout the night we were pitching and rolling, pitching and rolling.

I wasn't the only one who got sick that night. Most passengers were lying on couches or the floor, trying desperately to find some relief from seasickness. That was my first experience of the *mal de mer*. And from that point on, I wanted nothing to do with boats on water.

That was the moment that my fear was conceived, gestated, and birthed. All in one hop across the English Channel. Could I have avoided this fear from growing into a full-fledged fear of going out on boats? Perhaps.

Here's how I've learned to deal with fears that are in the process of being birthed: the more you remain conscious and aware *in the midst of* whatever event is creating the fear, the less of a hold that fear will have on you.

How do you stay conscious and aware? It's the same as the first step: interruption. So, in the example of my boats-on-water fear, if I had that first experience to do over, I would have done my best to notice the thoughts going through my head while I was seasick. I would have focused my attention on sensations and reminded myself that this discomfort was simply that—discomfort. It wasn't the end of the world (which is what my mind was screaming). That wouldn't have necessarily stopped the seasickness from playing itself out, **but it would have changed my relationship with it.**

At the end of that weekend, on the return trip, I would have done my best to remain super-conscious and aware on the boat. I didn't get sick on the way back, and

I would have made a point of reveling in my lack of sea-sickness—in feeling good while being at sea. I would have located in my body how good it felt to *not* be sick, and I would have deeply breathed in that awareness.

If I wanted to work further on it, later, on the safety of land, I could have brought to mind the feeling of being sick and practiced breathing and noticing how the memories made me feel in my body. I could have named my fear of going back out on a boat and thanked it for trying to protect me. And I could have called to mind and soaked in all of the great memories that were made possible by crossing the English Channel.

Having done all of this, I still may have chosen to limit my time on boats. The difference would be in my motivation. It would have been a choice based on knowledge and information rather than a phobic aversion based on fear.

As an endnote to that story, several years later when I was a senior in college, I participated in a five-week exchange program with the German Navy. I was assigned to a German frigate that was engaging in exercises in the North Sea . . . for TWO WEEKS. The North Sea is not a pond. It is a very active sea. With big waves.

I was standing with binoculars on the bridge of the frigate as we set sail, watching in dread as the lead ships in the squadron passed the breakwater. Huge plumes of sea spray shooting from their bows indicated rough waters ahead. Two weeks . . .

The first two days were tough. I did everything I could to keep my eyes trained on the horizon as I fought off the nausea. When my hosts tried to engage me in conversation in the galley, I only half listened as I did my best not to vomit my bratwurst all over the table.

But then something amazing happened. My seasickness left me. Completely. For the remainder of the cruise, I could be anywhere on the ship and be completely comfortable. It was kind of fun being up on the bridge in the stuffy, cramped navigation room trying to keep my balance as the boat rolled deeply to the left and right.

When we got back to port and I walked down the gangplank, I realized that I had developed my sea legs. I could barely keep my balance on the solid ground. It was such an odd feeling. I was elated to realize that I had not only survived the North Sea for two weeks, but I had actually enjoyed it.

This illustrates one more point about moving through these types of fears. Sometimes you might just need to "get back on the horse." If there really is an element of danger to that which you fear, make sure that you're safe when you decide to face it again, and always practice being aware and conscious throughout the experience. It may be that your fear is based on an irrational or illogical premise and that by going through the experience again (successfully), those premises fall away. This is referred to in psychology as "exposure therapy."

I still prefer to avoid boats on water, but I don't let that preference limit me from going out on a boat when there's a greater benefit, like being with friends, attending an important event that's being held on a boat, or seeing a place I really want to see that's only accessible by boat.

Daily Practices

None of the attitudes and habits I'm writing about come naturally. Or more accurately, they haven't come naturally to me and they haven't come naturally for many others I know and have worked with. It takes intention and a commitment to practicing daily.

I really like reading about extreme mountain climbing (from the comfort of my reading nook). When I first started reading stories about climbing Mount Everest, I was surprised to learn that no one climbs the mountain in one shot. My experience is limited to day hikes, and a one-shot climb is all I've ever done. You start, you climb, you reach the summit, you turn around, you climb back down. All before dinner.

Not so with Mount Everest (or any of the world's highest peaks). You end up climbing up the mountain multiple times, with each climb taking you higher. And after each climb, you return to base camp. Each climb acclimates you to higher and higher altitudes, and it also allows you to establish your supply chain.

On your final ascent, you climb to Camp Four. Camp Four is the point on Mount Everest at which you don't have enough oxygen to live—that is, you're slowly dying. They call it the "death zone." You spend the night, and before sun breaks the next day, you make your bid for the summit. Ideally you time it so that at this point, you're at your best in terms of acclimation.

I see dealing with fear in the same light. You can't just walk up to the fear mountain and climb it in one fell swoop. You have to build up your muscle; you have to become acclimated. And you have to do that daily. You have to go to the gym and do your reps if you want to have a chance at breaking through to the flipside.

Throughout this book, I've mentioned practices that will help build your muscle. I'll summarize them here.

Developing a daily meditation practice is the basis for all this work. Meditating for as little as one minute a day can begin to build your muscles of observation and focusing attention. These are the muscles that are needed to recognize intrusive thoughts and the signs of fear when they're happening, and to interrupt your reactive patterns before they play themselves out. Meditation doesn't necessarily mean sitting in the lotus position with your thumb and forefinger touching (although it can). You can choose any activity that's relaxing and allows you to focus your attention on your thoughts.

Noticing your breathing—and noting the quality of your breathing—throughout the day is another way to build your muscle. This does a couple of things. First, it strengthens the part of you that observes, that's not caught up in the story. This is the part of you that will take you successfully through to the flipside. Second, it strengthens your relationship with your body. It takes you out of your mind and directs your attention to your body. This kind of **body awareness** is critical for dealing productively with fear.

Having a daily meditation practice and noticing the quality of your breathing builds to the practice of **living mindfully throughout your day**. Living mindfully means being aware of what's going on around you and within you as life happens. Another way of saying this is *staying present*.

Our thoughts are always trying to get us to live in some other place and time than here and now. Neuroscientists call the regions in the brain responsible for this mind-wandering as the default mode network. According to the science, we're taken out of the present reality in at least three distinct ways.

First, we can get caught up in thoughts about ourselves:

I'm the kind of person who [fill in the blank]. I don't like [fill in the blank]. I'm so sad [or afraid or angry, etc.], I could just [fill in the blank].

Second, we can get caught up in thoughts about others:

What does he think about me? What do I think about him? What is she feeling? Am I better than her? I don't like them.

Third, we can get caught up in thoughts about the past or future:

Why did that have to happen? I wish it had gone differently. Wasn't it better back then? What if [fill in the blank] happens? I can't wait for [fill in the blank] to happen.

All these forms of mind-wandering—of being taken out of the present—provide a playground for our fears to show up in force. And living mindfully is the antidote.

Let me give you an example of living mindfully in regard to one of my forms of mind-wandering. I do not like getting my blood taken. I have what doctors call a vasovagal response. When I get my blood drawn, my body reacts by a drop in heart rate and blood pressure.

My first experience of this was when I was a senior in high school, getting my blood drawn for my Navy physical. As the needle was doing its thing, I felt myself getting dizzy, and the next thing I knew I was on the floor with a nurse waving smelling salts over my nose.

I got poked so many times in the Navy that I became used to it. I haven't fainted since, but periodically I feel myself getting clammy and dizzy. Regardless, my thoughts have a heyday in the days prior to getting my blood drawn. If I'm not mindful, I'm constantly thinking about the upcoming blood-letting, and I find myself getting tense and anxious. It takes me away from whatever is happening in the moment.

Mindfulness has changed my relationship with getting my blood drawn. When I catch myself thinking about the needle, I take a deep, conscious breath, and I say to myself: *There's nothing wrong with this moment.*

This moment is perfect. And it's true. **The only thing that's causing me anxiety in the moment is my thinking about some future moment.**

When I awake the morning of The Event, I repeat my mantra. As I'm walking to the lab near where I live, I look around at the trees and the sky and I breathe it all in. I remind myself, *I'm not in the chair right now. I'm walking, and it's a beautiful day. This moment is perfect.*

And when I'm sitting in the waiting room flipping through *People* magazine (I allow myself this guilty pleasure when I'm in a doctor's office) and my anxious thoughts try to zoom ahead, I repeat my mantra: *There's nothing wrong with this moment.*

When I'm in the chair and I get the sickening feeling as the giant rubber band cuts off my circulation, same thing: *There's nothing wrong with this moment.*

And when the needle goes in (and this is where it gets a little tricky): *There's nothing wrong with this moment. I'm experiencing a pricking sensation. A little pain. But there's nothing wrong with this moment. It's just a sensation, like anything else.* When my anxious thoughts try to wrestle control from me as my life force is being drained from my veins, I take a deep breath and repeat: *There's nothing wrong with this moment.*

In that moment of mild pain, my mind tries to label the sensation as "suffering." And in that act of labeling, it indeed becomes suffering. If my mind takes over, it turns pain into suffering, and then I do all I can to avoid it (my fear reaction). But if I stay with the sensation, noticing that it's mildly uncomfortable, but stopping there, I'm able to remain calm.

I've used this same practice with fearful and anxious thoughts that accompany unpleasant future events of all kinds. For example, The People Pleaser still shows up in my life when conflict arises. But now that my relationship with that fear has changed, I'm able to approach conflict differently.

When I sense that conflict is on the horizon, I notice my immediate tendency to anticipate and obsess about how the other might act or what they might say. I notice myself begin to lose touch with my truth as my fear activates my self-protection mode. I notice my sense of well-being diminish as I look outside myself for affirmation and validation.

When I notice these things, I ground myself in *this moment*. I breathe. I notice what's around me. And I thank The People Pleaser for trying to protect me, reminding myself that all is well. I go do something active and that I enjoy like taking a walk or working in the yard. And as I do those things, I continue my practice of being present to and aware of *this moment*—my breath, my body sensations, what's around me. When I do this, resolution to the conflict can come unexpectedly and without a lot of hand-wringing effort.

You see, it's only when we're present to this moment, right now, that we're able to come up with authentic, creative, and innovative solutions. When we're caught up in obsessive, fearful thoughts about the future, we're cut off from ourselves and our source of creativity.

When I'm not consumed by the fear, I'm much more tuned in to what I know to be true *and* to what the other person is actually saying or doing. I'm dealing in the world of reality rather than a world of perception created by my fear-based filters. And resolution is much quicker and more complete in the real world than in a perceived world.

The People Pleaser will likely continue to try to get my attention, but he feels much less powerful and compelling now, especially since I've identified the flipside regarding The People Pleaser:

> *I'm ready to get my sense of well-being from my own inner source. I'm ready to simply be me. And this authenticity will enrich my connection with others.*

Living an Inspired Life

Living on the flipside is really all about living an inspired life. An inspired life is a life that's governed by possibility and desire rather than external expectations or perceived obligations. There's an easy way to determine which side of the fear equation you're living on—the front side or the flipside. Pay attention to how much you use words like "should," "have to," and "ought." These are red flag indicators that you're living on the front side—limited and governed by fear.

On the other hand (or the other side), words like "want," "would like," and "desire" are indicators that you're living in a state of inspiration—on the flipside.

First, simply notice which words you use most frequently throughout the day. Next, see if you can catch yourself right before you use a fear word. Finally, see if you can replace your fear words with flipside words. This simple practice can help you remain on the flipside.

Have you heard of "being in flow?" Being in flow is living in a state of inspiration, when you're guided and directed by your sixth sense, your intuition. Your intuition is immune to your fears. Your intuition is that inner guidance system that gently nudges you in the direction of your dreams and desires. It directs your attention to people and things that "coincidentally" end up being exactly what you need at that moment to take the next step.[10]

Fear can never shut down that voice—it simply doesn't have the power to do so. However, fear can create interference in the line so that you can't hear the voice of intuition. Deal with the interference (through the three steps), and your intuition voice will begin to come to you more frequently and clearly.

This is the state of being that we're aiming for—a playful way of living that's full of eager anticipation for what's coming, for what's around the next corner, while at the same time fully experiencing what's in front of you.

I remember having this orientation to life when I was young. But somewhere in early high school—14 or 15—

this sense of wonder started to fade for me. My fears began to find their voices around this tender age of a rapidly changing body, increased peer pressure, and external definitions of "success" from teachers, coaches, and other adults in my life. I progressed through the rest of high school and college paying more and more attention to these external expectations. Meanwhile my Fearberg's "Storyline"—my belief ecosystem—was growing deeper and deeper below the water line.

If we don't address this state of dis-ease, each successive decade brings a deeper sense of purposelessness and numbness. We've all seen examples of what this leads to in later years—people who are caricatures of their worst traits, relationships that are severely taxed or completely severed, and daily lives that revolve around life-numbing rather than life-giving routines.

This doesn't have to happen to you and it doesn't have to happen to me! We have a choice. We have agency. We can do something about it. We can enter into flow and begin living our lives with less effort. Let me show you how this way of living led to me writing this book.

I co-lead workshops at Kripalu, a retreat center in western Massachusetts for people who want to take their craft or their passion and create their own workshops—transformational workshops. (Yes, it's a workshop on creating workshops.) In one of the workshops, a five-day workshop, we have the participants create and present their own 30-minute "mini-workshop" to a small group of others in the class. If the class doesn't have an even number of people, then one or more of the instructors must step into a group.

This happened recently—two groups needed an extra person. The question was posed: "Which two of us will step into the exercise?" I felt that feeling in my gut—what's becoming more and more clear to me as the voice of intuition: *Do it, David. This is what you need right now.*

And then another voice (I think it may have been The Couch Potato):

What?? This is your only free evening, and you're going to spend it planning a presentation for to-morrow from scratch? You're so tired and spent. Don't you just want to relax—take a walk, take a nap, read a book?

And there was another voice, the fear of failure:

But you don't have anything prepared! What if you can't come up with something? What if you do and it falls flat?

I felt in my body all the signs of my intuition coming up against my fear—butterflies in my stomach, tingling in my hands. And in that moment I was able to articulate the flipside of these fears:

I'm ready to take risks, be vulnerable, and put my-self out there. I'm ready to do the work I've been given to do.

I swallowed hard, raised my hand, and said, "I'll do it," even though I had no idea what topic I would present.

That afternoon I took a walk and let my mind wander over the topics I could develop into a 30-minute mini-workshop. My mind wandered right into the process I had been practicing for finding the flipside of my fears, and I decided that would be a good topic.

It was in preparing my mini-workshop that I first clarified the process that evolved into the three steps. And the next day, I led my small group through the process.

It was quick, but it was profound. The people in my group were struck by the movement they felt after going through the steps with a particular fear in mind. And I felt excited and fulfilled to have been able to put my process into practice and see others benefit.

And that's how this book was born. It was a completely unexpected extension of the flipside I articulated at Kripalu. Everything along the way since then has been fueled by inspiration. Circumstances have fallen into place, and the right people have come into my life at just the right time. And it all hinged on that moment of fear— give in and react, or interrupt it, approach it, and flip it into a new way of being.

And this is exactly the gift of fear. **In that moment, my fear was an indication to me that I was at a crossroads.** I could either choose the very well-worn fear-driven path or I could choose the other way—the inspired way. The gift of my fear in that moment was its revelation that there was a flipside right around the corner, if I chose to go there. It was showing me that I had come to a doorway that led to growth and expansion in my journey.

Choosing the Flipside

It's so important to pay attention to both these voices: Our voice of intuition that tugs at our heart *and* the voice of fear that shows us we're rubbing up against the edge of our comfort zone. By paying attention, we're awake at that crucial decision point. We can exercise *choice*—take the inspired way or take the reactive fight, flight, or freeze way.

But I don't always choose the inspired way. I sometimes react rather than respond. And I still find my mind wandering. When I come to the crossroads, I sometimes choose the well-worn, comfortable path. And that's o.k. We're not always ready to move from the front side to the flipside of fear. The beauty of life is that we always get another chance. Yes, circumstances will be different the next time around, and sometimes there are painful consequences that result from remaining in our fear. But life will continue to present opportunities right at the edge of our comfort zone. Thank goodness that life is relentless that way.

A gifted healer and mentor of mine, Lauri Sowers, once said to me, "When you feel the voice of inspiration, take one little step in its direction." When we do this over and over again, we strengthen our connection to our intuition—our inspired voice—and it becomes easier and easier. Over time we find that these little steps have taken us down the roadway of inspired living. This is the way I want to live!

I'm thankful and grateful for fear. It heightens our senses and our awareness, and it opens up the possibility that there's more to life than avoiding the things that make us uncomfortable. It points to a new way of showing up in the world—the flipside. Consider making it your daily practice to wake up and stay awake, to listen to your body for the first signs of fear, and to explore it for the flipside that's always there. It's ours to find. It's ours to explore. And it's ours to live.

A Note to the Reader

Thank you, dear reader, for accompanying me on this journey. This book was a joy to write, and I hope reading it has helped you get closer to the flipside. As you may know, reader reviews are one of the most powerful ways that books and readers find each other. I would very much appreciate your honest review on Amazon and Goodreads.

Please visit my website (www.davidronka.com) to find resources that will help you explore your fears and their flipside. To help you put the three steps into practice, I'm offering a **free, downloadable "Flipside Worksheet"**—a PDF document with prompts and space to write in your reflections for each of the three steps:

www.davidronka.com/the-flipside-of-fear

End Notes

Chapter 1, Exploring Fear

1 **"In my experience, however, there are really only two basic emotions. There's fear and there's love. Everything in between is some combination of the two."** Christian scripture seems to point to this fear-love continuum. The apostle John points out that love and fear are mutually exclusive: "There is no fear in love. But perfect love drives out fear . . ." (1 John 4:18, New International Version). Esther Hicks also uses this continuum of fear and love to describe the full range of human emotions in her many books about the Law of Attraction. Authors Gary Zukav and Linda Francis, in their book *The Heart of the Soul*, put forth two ends of the continuum: fear/doubt and love/trust. They explain that energy enters the body's energy system, circulates, and leaves the body as either fear/doubt or love/trust.

Our emotions become the classroom of life, showing us where it is that we are being called to grow. And Michael Singer, in his book *The Untethered Soul*, writes that "Fear is the cause of every problem. It's the root of all prejudices and the negative emotions of anger, jealousy, and possessiveness."

2 **"We both had been practicing manifestation (the art of creating in your life what you desire in your heart), so we decided to get serious (and playful) about it by dreaming about what that might look and feel like."** This process for manifestation is based on the belief that we have agency in what reality presents to us, and by changing our beliefs and emotional states, we can attract more of what we want into our lives. I've seen significant congruence and corroboration of this concept from very diverse fields of knowledge: quantum physics, psychology, neuroscience, spirituality/religion, and metaphysics. The Law of Attraction, as expressed by Abraham-Hicks, has been the most helpful articulation of the how-to for me, but there are examples and models in each of those fields.

3 **"I had the presence of mind and the support from close friends and family at the time to recognize the discomfort and to resist the urge to numb or distract myself while going through the process of separation and divorce."** In addition to friends and family, several books were life savers in moving through my divorce productively and in such a transformational

way: *Transitions* (William Bridges); *Broken Open* (Elizabeth Lesser); *The Heart of the Soul* (Gary Zukav and Linda Francis); *Spiritual Divorce* (Debbie Ford); and *When Things Fall Apart* (Pema Chödrön).

4 "Do you recognize your fear in any of those [Enneagram-related] statements? If so, can you put some specifics to it? When's the last time you felt this fear? How intense was it? What triggered it, and how did you react?" There are many resources on the web for determining your type and learning more about the Enneagram model. The Enneagram Institute is one that I turn to frequently. Also, the Enneagram in Business website provides powerful resources for applying the Enneagram model to the world of work. Please refer to:

www.enneagraminstitute.com
www.theenneagraminbusiness.com

Chapter 2, The Flipside of Fear

5 "I'm also acknowledging that there's the rest of me—the me that exists apart from my fear—that isn't afraid and that knows how to respond wisely." Internal Family Systems (IFS), developed by Dr. Richard Schwartz, is a model that clearly articulates this idea that there are many parts of us, called "sub-personalities." There's much more to the model than can be explained here, but it describes our psyche as consisting of many interacting parts, all wanting to play a valuable role within the whole. The model divides these parts into three categories: managers, protectors, and exiles. In addition to these parts, there's also a Self, different from the parts. The goal of IFS is to differentiate the Self from the parts and for the Self to dialog with the parts, helping them return to their original roles from their more extreme roles (which often came about from some form of trauma). This idea of parts and a Self is also articulated in other psychological models, such as Freud's psychoanalytic theory (id, ego, and super ego), object relations theory, transactional analysis, and some cognitive-behavioral models.

Chapter 3, Step 1: Interrupt Fear

6 **"By mastering our breath, we're able to deactivate the SNS and activate the PNS, and this switch is all it takes to move from reacting to responding."** While there are many sources that discuss this concept scientifically, I'm also very interested in the spiritual connections to breath. In many of the world's major religions, breath is inextricably tied to God and the source of life. For example, in the Jewish, Hindu, Christian, and Muslim traditions, it's God's breath that animates humans. And it's our own breath that fills us with life. Stop breathing, stop living. Neil Douglas-Klotz, in his book *Prayers of the Cosmos*, provides a translation of the Lord's prayer from Aramaic—Jesus' spoken language—where the first phrase of the prayer ("Our Father who art in heaven" in English, which is *Abwoon d'bwashmaya*

phonetically in Aramaic) is, "Respiration of all worlds, we hear you breathing—in and out—in silence." He poetically imagines this breath of God being exchanged in perfect harmony between mammals and plants—oxygen and carbon dioxide exchanging places in a dance that gives ongoing life to the whole world. David Deida, one of my favorite relationship authors, likens the in-breath to our first breath as an infant and the out-breath to our last dying breath. In this way, each breath we take replicates the full cycle of life. These connections between breath and life in both wisdom traditions and science have important implications for us as we seek to interrupt our fear reaction. Breath has great power—power to connect us to ourselves, to the world around us, and to the divine.

7 **"I began to see meditation like lifting weights. Competitive athletes who lift weights as part of their training don't do so to become better weight lifters (unless their sport is weight lifting, of course). Rather, they lift weights so that their bodies are conditioned to perform to their highest potential in the game."** I first had this thought about equating noticing mind-wandering to weight-lifting reps in a gym when I experienced the connection between noticing my mind wandering in meditation and noticing my mind wandering as I went about my day. It was a major ah-ha moment for me, and it totally changed my perspective on meditation. As I read more about meditation, I saw other authors explain it in similar ways:

meditation as a practice in noticing rather than being a way to induce a "meditative state." I would have been saved many hours of frustrated meditation experience had I realized this sooner. But that's part of the journey, too, isn't it?

8 "Practices such as meditation and body awareness have helped me become more conscious, aware, awake, and present." I've been aided in my journey to greater presence and awareness by books from ancient wisdom traditions, including Buddhism and Christian mysticism (authors Pema Chödrön and Richard Rohr, for example), as well as more modern expressions of ancient wisdom (authors Eckhart Tolle and Wayne Dyer, for example).

Chapter 5, Step 3: Flip Fear

9 "This was a freedom experienced within the context of responsibility and constraint. This was a freedom that would allow me to live a more purposeful and inspired life, entering into commitments and making promises to the world that I fully intended to keep. And that's how I wanted to live from now on! That was my inspired way. As often happens, I was helped in this awareness by a wise teacher. David Deida and his writings about masculinity and freedom helped me to articulate the flipside of The Freedom Fighter." Author David Deida approaches relationship dynamics from an energetic perspective, rather than a strictly gender- or role-based perspective. He first introduced me to this idea of intrinsic freedom in a workshop I took, and he articulates it well in his book, *Intimate Communion*. He posits that the masculine seeks the energy of freedom and purpose while the feminine seeks the energy of love and connection. (We all have a mix of masculine and feminine, and these don't necessarily always correlate with male and female.) Deida has very strong opinions and can tend to be edgy and provocative. These qualities have helped dislodge some of my very ingrained, traditional ways of thinking about men and women and relationships.

Chapter 6, Living on the Flipside of Fear

10 "Have you heard of "being in flow?" Being in flow is living in a state of inspiration, when you're guided and directed by your sixth sense, your intuition. Your intuition is immune to your fears. Your intuition is that inner guidance system that gently nudges you in the direction of your dreams and desires. It directs your attention to people and things that "coincidentally" end up being exactly what you need at that moment to take the next step." Hungarian psychologist Mihaly Csikszentmihalyi, credited with recognizing and naming the concept of Flow, once said, "Repression is not the way to virtue. When people restrain themselves out of fear, their lives are by necessity diminished. Only through freely chosen discipline can life be enjoyed and still kept within the bounds of reason." He describes Flow as an "effortless and spontaneous" state of being that accompanies people who are successful and happy at work and play.

Acknowledgements

S ometimes when I read the acknowledgements section in a book it feels a little like I'm intruding on the author's private world. There are inside jokes, names I don't recognize, tasks for which people are being thanked that I had no idea were part of writing a book. Now, as I sit down to acknowledge and thank those who have helped me in this process, I realize how vulnerable it can feel to put "thank you" to paper, especially when you risk forgetting someone. There are so many who have been part of my journey . . .

I'd like to acknowledge the wealth of insight and inspiration I've received from the authors, teachers, and healers I've met along the way. What I've learned in my journey is that the miracle of transformation is sparked and fueled by a few basic elements. These can be expressed and experienced in multiple forms. But every method, approach, technique, or description of transformation seems to come down to these things: mindfulness, self-awareness, non-judgment, breathing, and allowing (and I could keep on listing similar words).

Where my thoughts were inspired or informed by a specific person or book, I've tried to give credit and provide some context—within the text or with endnotes. My sincere apologies where I may have inadvertently failed in this intention. My website (www.davidronka.com) contains a resource section with a more comprehensive list of books and TED talks that have helped me in my journey.

I'd also like to thank the many members of my "launch team." This group of people encouraged me along the way and provided me with valuable feedback. My launch team included: Alastair Kirk, Alix Ronka, Ben Leeming, Beth Ronka, Bobby Greene, Cari Pattison, Colleen Burns, JC Alfonso, Jeffrey Schra, Jim Ronka, Julie Meltzer, Katanna Conley, Kate Theriault, Katie Atkinson, Kim Knox, Lauri Sowers, Paul Ronka, Peter Matz, Stan Smith, Stefanie Haug, Stephanie Murray, Stephen Dyball, Sylvia Vogt, Tim Williams, and Yvonne Jones. Thank you also to those who joined the team later, and aren't mentioned here by name, including the Self-Publishing School (SPS) community and those from SPS who supported my launch.

A special thanks to those who spent a considerable amount of extra time reviewing and providing feedback on various versions of the manuscript: Jim Ronka (who missed his calling as an editor!), Colleen Burns, Peter Matz, Julie Meltzer, Stephanie Murray, Ben Leeming, and Susan Leeming. Their insight and suggestions helped refine my thinking, clarify my wording, and get rid of stuff that just wasn't important. A special thanks to my big sister, Katie Atkinson, for her creativity consulting and for designing such a beautiful cover.

I wrote that I co-lead workshops at Kripalu. My deep gratitude goes to my fellow co-leaders: Ken Nelson and Lesli Lang, who lead the work, and Liz Korabek-Emerson and Jim White, who, along with me, help Ken and Lesli. Ken and Lesli have developed a powerful series of workshops that help healers and leaders bring their work and their passion to the world in the form of transformational workshops. I've benefitted greatly from co-leading these workshops, and much of what I've written around mindfulness, awareness, and "flipping" painful emotions is also articulated in some form in Ken and Lesli's work. Liz specifically helped me the night before my mini-workshop by masterfully guiding me as I pulled thoughts from my brain to articulate the flipside process. And Jim's passion for and research into the science behind individual and group behavior has helped me better understand the "why," including the default mode network that I referred to. My gratitude and admiration go to Ken, Lesli, Liz, and Jim for the important work they do in helping people be agents of transformation.

I'm grateful for my family and dear friends, who have walked alongside me the past few years of life transition—from leaving my full-time job, through divorce, to exploring new possibilities for my life's work, to finding new love (and a lot of other stuff in between). I wouldn't be where I am today without their kindness and compassion, willingness to listen, and timely words of wisdom. I won't list them all by name; they know who they are. I will, however, thank Alix Ronka, my sister, by name. She was with me in the midst of the fear storm related to moving in with my girlfriend. Alix helped me tease out the set of fears I wrote about, which was aided by coffee, a crackling fire, and two cats that provided for moments of laughter and levity as I approached my fears. And I thank my parents, Paul and Beth Ronka. They've served as consistent and reliable mentors, thought partners, supporters, and comforters, particularly in my journey through divorce and into the second half of my life. They've listened to me try to articulate my evolving view of life, patiently and compassionately bearing with me in both my confusion and sense of certainty.

Over these past few years of major life transitions I've assembled what I call "Team Ronka." In addition to family and friends, Team Ronka is made up of mentors, teachers, and healers who each support me in some critical way. I'd like to mention two here, because their wisdom and compassion helped me through some very dark times, and much of what I've articulated in this book came in one way or another from them. Liz Turner and Lauri Sowers have both spent countless hours listening to me try to make sense of whatever dark cave I felt I was trapped in. They have my deep gratitude and admiration for their encouragement and keen insight.

And I'm especially grateful to my girlfriend and partner, Sonia, whom I've referenced throughout the book.

ACKNOWLEDGEMENTS

Thank you, Sonia, for accompanying me on this journey, fears and all, and thank you for your support and insight throughout writing this book. Thank you for the gift of your presence, and thank you for being you and encouraging me to be me. Here's to living life on the flipside!

About the Author

David Ronka is passionate about helping people navigate through life's passages. He draws from his diverse background as teacher, management consultant, life coach, one-time expatriate, civil engineer, Naval Officer, musician, and artist. David holds a Master of Education from Harvard University and a B.A. (German) and B.S. (Civil Engineering) from Tufts University. He is a contributing author of *Data Wise in Action: Stories of Schools Using Data to Improve Teaching and Learning*. David lives with his partner on the southern coast of Maine.

·

www.ingramcontent.com/pod-product-compliance
Lightning Source LLC
Chambersburg PA
CBHW061830040426
42447CB00012B/2908